# THERE AND BACK AGAIN

## America Through the Eyes of a Traveling Veterans' Disability Attorney

### JUNE 2019 — MARCH 2020

## TYLER C. HADYNIAK

# THERE AND BACK AGAIN: AMERICA THROUGH THE EYES OF A TRAVELING VETERANS' DISABILITY ATTORNEY

1405 SW 6th Avenue • Ocala, Florida 34471 • Phone 352-622-1825 • Fax 352-622-1875
Website: www.atlantic-pub.com • Email: sales@atlantic-pub.com
SAN Number: 268-1250

Library of Congress Control Number: 2020919991

Printed in the United States

PROJECT MANAGER: Kassandra White
INTERIOR LAYOUT AND JACKET DESIGN: Nicole Sturk

# ACKNOWLEDGMENTS

---

Getting a client to a Board of Veterans' Appeals hearing requires far more than just the hearing itself. To that end, I want to thank the entire staff at Jackson and MacNichol. It certainly takes a team to provide quality representation. Everyone — case managers, interns, support staff, and my fellow attorneys — devote their workdays to making sure veterans get the attention they deserve. Without this office's help the traveling attorney's job is impossible. In a way, much of my work is done when a veteran gets to his hearing. The bases are already loaded, I just have to get a base hit. The folks at the firm are all a part of the machine that makes that happen. My sincere thanks for their hard work and dedication.

Finally, this is my first book, and I could not have had a better publishing house than Atlantic Publishing. They made the process easy, fun, and provided the support on the way to make this book as full of potential as possible. Special thanks to my editor, Kassandra White, and the wonderful folks who designed the layout, pictures, and tackled the marketing and distribution.

# DEDICATION

It would be cliché for me to start a dedication section with "There are too many people to list." Regardless, such is the case. I am immeasurably thankful for the unique, profound impact everyone has had on my life. I truly believe any one person is a culmination of influences. Beyond their general influences, I can think of many specific life lessons.

A special shout out to my mother, who would encourage my brother and I from an early age to write, write, write (and write well — she would correct Dr. Seuss' abhorrent grammar). To my father, who instilled a sense of travel when we would road-trip around the southeastern United States, visiting Civil War battlefields. It's not a coincidence that I combined these two strong memories from each parent and now write about my travels.

My wife, Catherine, deserves special mention as well. Neither she nor I truly knew what I was getting myself into when I accepted this job in March 2018. At that point we had only been dating for a few weeks. She knew that my professional life, for the next couple years, at least, would involve me being away from home for long periods of time. However, I don't think either of us anticipated that my travels would be so dense. Thankfully, we did not have kids, and she was still in nursing school, so if there was any time to be away from home, it would be then. Despite this understanding, being separated was tough. Many of my happy reflections could be amended with the addendum, *"and despite this, I so missed Catherine."* But she knew how important this work was for me, and I told her right from the beginning that, "I will not do this job, in this form, when we have kids. That would not be fair to you, them, or me." As it turns out, my travels abruptly ended not because of kids but because of the COVID-19 virus.

When I started this journal, I had two surviving grandparents. By the time of publication, only one remained. My maternal grandfather, Norm Qualtrough, served his country in an Army uniform for 30 years, retiring as a "full-bird" colonel. He served two decorated tours in Vietnam. As I elaborate over the course of this book, we maintained, and still maintain, a strong relationship despite living 600 miles apart. We communicate often by phone. I will always cherish the talks we had about my travels and my job. He was *the* strong influence in me getting into the veterans' disability field. He also was the first to encourage me to publish this book. My job, my travels, and this book would not have happened but for his influence.

My paternal grandmother, Sallyann, was always my number one cheerleader. She was the family personality; a beloved member of the Freedom, Maine, community; and the single strongest influence in my life. Everything I ever do should be perpetually dedicated to her. She could never contain her pride for either of her grandchildren. I still laugh when I remember one time at a local restaurant shortly after I passed the bar, she proudly introduced me to a friend as "my grandson, Tyler Charles Hadyniak, *attorney at law.*" She wrote the Republican Journal's Freedom town column for almost 20 years. After she passed away on November 5, 2019, my family found one of her articles that she kept in a desk drawer. It was the article where she proudly announced that her grandson had passed the bar. Viscerally patriotic and a Navy veteran's widow, she was incredibly proud of my work helping veterans. She bought me the map I used to track my hearing locations and road trip routes and kept one for herself, always getting on my case to update her on my travels, so she in turn could fastidiously update her map. I feel like in a way only a recovered 20-year agoraphobic could appreciate, she lived vicariously through my stories, pictures, and this map. More could be written, but not enough can be said.

# TABLE OF CONTENTS

*Map of My Travels*

# FOREWORD

———◆◆◆———

Tyler Hadyniak is a contradiction. He is man who was born in urban New Jersey but was brought to Maine by his parents at a young age. He grew up in a classic small town in Freedom, Maine but moved to Maine's largest city, Portland, to attend law school. He and his wife have moved to another small town, Sidney, Maine, but he loves travelling to Southwest vistas and elsewhere.

However, there is no contradiction in his love of veterans' law. That in turn is an outgrowth of his love of military history, especially the history of the American Civil War. Tyler has tramped many of the Civil War's battlefields. His grandfather, a veteran himself, explored many of those battle sites with Tyler.

The book that follows is a narrative of his extensive travels, frequently several days per week, many weeks per year, across much of America, in search of justice for veterans who have suffered disabilities that stem from their military service.

Many veterans suffer from physical disabilities. Some are specific to particular wars, such as the cold injuries of those who fought in Korea, or the Agent Orange related conditions suffered by those who served in Vietnam on land and in the ships stationed offshore. A younger generation suffers from Gulf War syndrome or the exposure to the horrific burn pits used by the military. Others suffer from invisible mental scars. What all have in common is a need for expert help from lawyers like Tyler in obtaining the disability compensation promised them by Congress, but frequently not delivered by the slow moving bureaucracy that is now the Department of Veterans' Affairs.

While much of Tyler's writing is a narrative of interesting and beautiful parts of the United States, there is much more. His narrative also includes introspective comments on his state of mind as he grew from a neophyte to an experienced veterans attorney. Interwoven through all of that are his comments on the veterans who he represented, helping them to present their claims to the judges of the Board of Veterans' Appeals at veterans facilities located throughout the country – locations ranging from the metropolitan to the bucolic. It contains a fascinating interweaving of the enjoyment of travel and introspective comments on personal growth and direction, all interspersed with glimpses into the day to day struggles faced by many of our veterans.

It is hard to remember that prior to the establishment of the Court of Appeals for Veterans Claims, created by an Act of Congress in 1988, there was no direct appeal to any court from denials of benefits by what was then the Veterans Administration (now the Department of Veterans Affairs). At that time there were few attorneys in the nation focusing on issues relating to veterans. I have had the privilege of seeing the Court develop from its first cases in 1990, filing my own first case there in 1991 with oral argument and a decision in 1992. That case, *Smith v. Derwinski*, 2 Vet.App. 241 (1992), was at a time when the court was so new that there were very few precedents. Now the Court has over 30 volumes of precedent.

In 1993, NOVA (the National Organization of Veterans Advocates) was formed with an introductory meeting in Arlington, Virginia of a handful of attorneys. I was fortunate enough to attend that meeting and have now been a member for over 25 years. Since 1993, veterans benefits law has grown dramatically, now with several law firms having multiple attorneys, like Tyler, who devote their entire legal practice to helping veterans to get justice. For many years, like Tyler, I had the opportunity to travel to various VA facilities and participate in hearings. Although I now restrict my practice to cases at the Court of Appeals for Veterans Claims, I have fond memories of several such trips (as well as less fond memories such as a trip to New Orleans in July with the temperature over 100 and the humidity at 99 percent).

What is important, however, is that Tyler is representative of the new breed of VA attorneys. We are fortunate enough in our office to have an entire group of dedicated and hardworking attorneys striving every day to get justice for veterans. This justice is well-earned.

by Francis M. Jackson

# A NOTE ABOUT THIS JOURNAL
# AND MY TRAVELS

———◆◆◆———

A couple important notes before you, the reader, start this journal. First, you will see that many of my work trips resulted in personal excursions, ranging from as small as a museum visit to as big as a 1,900-mile road trip. Please understand: These excursions were at entirely my cost. I *never* charged the firm for an expense that was not client-related. If an expense could be applied to both personal and work purposes — rental cars immediately come to mind — I would prorate my reimbursement request. For example, if I used a rental car for work two days in a row and then for personal use on the third day, I would ask to be reimbursed for only 66 percent of the rental car cost.

Secondly, I always kept in mind that I was traveling for work. Work came first, my own recreation second. Sometimes I had to forgo opportunities because I had to stay in the hotel room to do work. I traveled with my work computer and had full access to the firm's software. As often as I would sit in airport terminals and sleep, read, or watch TV, I would also be able to log into my work computer and get some work done. All this said, when I was in Maine and in the office, I would work like hell to get my hearing preparation complete, so I did not have to do so much on the road.

Finally, I originally wrote this journal based on the advice of my grandfather: write as if I will be the only one to ever read it. Such secrecy would allow me to be true to myself, recollections, and observations. Therefore, you can be assured that I have *not* edited my journal for dramatic purposes. I added some detail, narration, changed tenses, and changed names of clients, but otherwise everything you see is true to my experiences. Maybe when you turn the last page you will conclude this book was boring, maybe not. You might ask, "Who the hell cares?" or "What makes him so special?" I had to ask myself these same questions when I decided to look for publishers. I pulled the trigger on this book because I thought I had a truly meaningful, unique story to tell, and I would leave it up to the individual reader to determine if my writing was boring, if they cared about my travels, or if they think my story is special. More than making money off this book, I want it to be appreciated and well-received. I also want it to be a continued method of my advocacy for disabled veterans. That's why at least half of my profits from sales will go to a national veterans' charity.

# PROLOGUE

In March 2018, my boss, Francis "Jack" Jackson, offered me a position at his law firm as a full-time traveling attorney, contingent on passing the state bar exam. I was finishing my third year at the University of Maine School of Law, had no children, had only been seeing my now-wife for a couple weeks, and had no other job lined up after school. I had been working at his law firm since June 2017 as an intern and had grown to love the field of veterans' disability — the area of law where attorneys help military veterans get compensation benefits from the Department of Veterans Affairs. I was heavily inspired to start working in the field by my Vietnam veteran grandfather, Norm, with whom I love talking about the work I did. As a traveling attorney, my job would be to fly around the country and represent these veterans before Veterans' Law Judges.

I did not have to consider Jack's job offer for long. Opportunity to travel? Autonomous work environment? A wonderful sense of fulfillment? Oral advocacy? Sign me up! I heartily accepted, but realized I had one unavoidable hump to get over, the bane of all law students' existence: the bar exam. But I had a study plan, professional programs to help study, and the necessary time off of my intern work. What stood in my way?

The answer to that was eight-tenths of a point. That's right — I failed the July 2018 bar exam by eight-tenths of a point. I was crushed, despondent, embarrassed — pick any adjective you like to describe what it means to be spiritually and emotionally destroyed. I had studied 10 hours a day, five or six days a week since graduation in May. How could I have committed myself so much and come up so short? I was suddenly left rudderless, watching the job opportunity I was so looking forward to disappear out of view.

I decided I would take the exam only once more. With the encouragement of friends and family, I rallied my spirits and crafted a study plan. From September 2018 to February 2019, I studied for four hours in the morning in my office — usually from 6:15 a.m. until around lunch — and then went "on the clock" until 5 p.m. I still shudder at the memory of leaving my Westbrook, Maine, apartment before the crack of dawn, fighting bitter cold and a car that didn't start half the time. I would always be the first one in the office. I closed my door, lowered my window shutters, and concentrated on legal material I knew I had no interest in practicing. But I needed that coveted bar certification. The three years I worked hard in law school deserved one more try. Otherwise, what were those three years worth?

I kept a disciplined schedule — four hours a day, no more, no less. One 10-minute break to walk around the parking lot and listen to music, trying to clear my mind before I took the next practice test. Bar study did not become my life like it did the first time around, but it weighed down my life in a way that, unfortunately, it does for most law school graduates. I clearly remember getting off work and driving over to the gym, where I would run out the frustration that I had nowhere to aim but at myself. Rinse and repeat, every workday for six months. I was sure I was not going to pass again, thereby wasting months of my life, thousands of dollars, and precluding myself from embarking on the career I wanted before it even began. Besides the harsh reality of not passing the test, I felt like I had disappointed everyone I knew, and I had personally embarrassed myself. And all of my anger was directed at me, for I could blame no one else for my failure.

I sat for the bar in North Dakota, which I am not ashamed to say I picked because it had the lowest passing threshold of all states that administered the Uniform Bar Exam. Generously, Jack not only gave me a second chance to pass the exam, but also paid for me to fly out to North Dakota and take it.

My hard work paid off when I learned in April 2019 that I passed the bar with a score 30 points higher than the first time I took it, thereby allowing me to apply my score for Maine Bar acceptance. What a joyous day! My discipline and despondency paid off once I got that congratulatory email. As the reader will see, it has already paid off a thousand times over since that day.

In April and May 2019 I waited with baited breath for my Department of Veterans Affairs certification to be approved — the last step to being able to "get on the road." North Dakota Bar license? Check. VA certification? Check. Then one day in May, the email from the office hearing coordinator came through and changed my life. I skimmed the first of many emails I would receive like this one, looking to see where I would be sent.

A nine-month, life-changing tour of the United States was about to begin. Over the next nine months and 143 pages, I would visit 40 states, have 77 different hearings, and be away from home one out of every three nights. The first stop on this whirlwind tour: Saint Paul, Minnesota, on June 6, 2019.

# JUNE 2019

———◆◆———

**FIRST WEEK OF JUNE, 2019:** This week saw my first hearings, in Saint Paul, Minnesota, and Winston-Salem, North Carolina. I spent hours trying to figure out what I could do around my hotel, in order to best live up visiting this city I had never been to before. I promised myself I was never going to just sit in my hotel room if there was something to do nearby. My free time was my own. Of course, I had to devote some time to hearing preparation, but my understanding was that I could do whatever I wanted off work hours.

It did not take long for me to realize what I wanted to do the night before my hearing — visit the Mall of America. My friends and family will attest to the fact that I abhor malls, but I thought it would be good to at least say I visited it once in my life. I walked the mile or so from my hotel to the mall. I walked in, and I immediately thought: "This damn thing has its own indoor amusement park!" Beyond that, it was like a little self-contained city. I had nothing like it growing up in rural Maine. Those who have visited it know how imposing it is. I could have never gone through the whole building if I weren't by myself.

To my surprise, I was nervous before the start of my hearing the next morning. I had observed my coworkers in hearings, and I thought I had a strong enough grasp on my client's case to warrant feeling at ease. I was taken aback when my client and I entered the hearing room to find a judge sitting at the table across from us. Most of these hearings before Board of Veterans' Appeals judges are via video conference; I had no reason to think such would not be the case here. Furthermore, the judge was one of the more senior members of the board, having held her job for at least a decade.

Despite this initial setback, I think I adequately rallied myself and argued my client's case well. The judge asked some tough questions that went toward the validity of the client's claims, but overall, I walked away from the 20-minute hearing satisfied I did well. My client was happy that he finally had his chance to address a judge. Like most of Jackson and MacNichol's client base, he was a Vietnam-era veteran in his late 60s. Rough around the edges with a "me against the world" mentality, but a little quirky — he told me about a nude beach in Minnesota he heartily endorsed. Did I ask him to tell me about Minnesota's premier nude beaches? Absolutely not.

I booked it from the VA regional office to the airport, flew through security (thanks to my TSA PreCheck clearance), and arrived at my gate 10 minutes before my plane took off. Too close for comfort! My next stop: Winston-Salem, North Carolina.

This leg of my trip was the first instance in this job of a life lesson I cherish: usually, *all it takes is the effort.* Want to do something you love? All it takes is the effort. Not sure you have time to visit that relative or make that phone call to keep in touch with a friend? All it takes is the effort. I had considerable time to kill in North Carolina, had already rented a car, and held a life-long interest in American battlefields. How did I reconcile the two? You got it — put in the effort! So I drove two hours out of my way to visit the Guilford Courthouse Military Park, the site of a decisive battle during the American Revolution, and the Bennett Place, the site of the largest Confederate surrender of the Civil War. I shed my hesitant nature and quickly acclimated to driving in unfamiliar places. Driving in central North Carolina, between two historical sites I had never visited before, I could tell right away I was going to love the autonomous travel aspect of this job, and it was moving to actually meet my clients. Since I started working at Jackson and MacNichol, they had only been names in files, but now that I got to put faces to names, my job became much more personal.

My North Carolina client was particularly memorable. He was a 40-something year old African American who hadn't been able to work since leaving the Army in 2000. He lived with his mother; she was his primary caretaker and did everything for him. She was devoted to his well-being and drove him to the hearing. I had to jump in the car with her and help her find parking before the hearing started. She was 70 years old, a smoker, terribly out of shape, and knew she wasn't going to be around forever to take care of her son. We had to stop every few steps between the parking garage and the hearing office, so she could catch her breath. The son was shy and obviously deferred to his mother's strong personality. It was blatantly obvious he would have a very hard time getting along in life without his mother. His PTSD and asthma were the primary cause of his inability to work. Here it was my job to convince the judge that this PTSD and asthma, already conceded as service connected, caused the veteran to be entirely unable to work. I knew that winning this client's case would relieve some of the strain on not only the client, but his mother and family as well. It was here I realized that my job had far more reaching implications than just helping one veteran on any given case.

Frequently, veterans' families depend on the veteran's disability income to buy food, put a roof over their heads, or feed their children. The pressure was on me to not let them down. I felt I had developed a close connection to this client and his mother, despite only knowing them for a grand total of maybe two hours. I helped the mother across the street, up the stairs, and into the hearing room. She was extremely worried about her son's well-being and wanted to support him in any way she could. I could not let them down. I couldn't let *her* down.

I returned home elated at how the first week went. I thought it was so exotic being able to travel to two different cities in one week. Soon enough, traveling to *only* two different cities in a week would be a nice, slow pace!

**SECOND WEEK OF JUNE, 2019:** This week I had a hearing in Brookings, Oregon. Brookings is a small coastal town near the California/Oregon border. Like many of my hearing locations, this was not at a VA regional office but at a VA medical satellite office. I erroneously thought it

16

was not close to any major airport, so I decided to fly into Portland, Oregon and drive down the Oregon coast. The plane ride out was about five hours long and afforded me the first taste of how much free time I would have on my hands while traveling. My cell phone quickly turned into my savior. On it I could read Kindle books, watch Hulu and Netflix, listen to music, and otherwise escape the monotony of long plane rides. But most efficient of all, I learned I could sleep anywhere, in any position. This was also unfortunate, as I suffer from recurrent sleep paralysis — a rare disorder that only about 5 percent of the population experiences as regularly as I do. When experiencing an "episode" you are conscious but unable to move. Thankfully, this afflicts me only when taking naps, not at night. In this semi-conscious state, you can imagine things that aren't there, a choking sensation, pressure on your chest, and all the while you are powerless to do anything about it. A person staring at you in the real world would have absolutely no idea what's going on. As I described to a friend, these episodes feel like toeing the line between the dream world and reality. It can be truly terrifying. Over the years, I have learned to recognize when I am experiencing "an episode" and have just learned to live with it and try to control the panic that sets in. Regardless and as time went on, I think my body literally trained itself to get tired as soon as I saw a plane passenger seat. I was on the West Coast in no time.

The drive to Brookings was six hours long. Much of it was stop-and-go, as I had to navigate tourists and visitors like myself, who flock to the Oregon coast for its scenic beauty. I determined the scenic beauty was much like what I was used to in Maine, making my much-hyped drive somewhat disappointing. I also was already somewhat familiar with that part of Oregon, as I drove up I-5 from northern California to Portland when I did a Portland, Maine, to Portland, Oregon, cross-country road trip during my third year of law school.

My client's hearing was via video conference with a judge in Washington, DC. The hearing turned contentious when the client's wife — who was as fed up with the VA process as everyone else was — made a snarky comment to the judge, earning the judge's rebuke. She was another example of how the fight to get disability compensation is far more than just about the veteran.

On my return trip to Portland I spent some time with my uncle, Evan, who had lived in Portland for the past few years. I went to dinner with him and his girlfriend. It was nice to see him, having seen him only twice in the past 13 years. This would prove to be a fun fringe benefit of work travel: visiting friends and family I would never get to see otherwise.

I rushed back home to Maine in time for my swearing-in to the Maine Bar on Friday, June 14, 2019. I could count this as one of the most momentous days of my life. It was the ultimate goal; Maine has such a high bar passage score that only those who perform exceptionally well on the bar exam get to become members of the Maine bar. After my disastrous first-time bar score, I thought I would never get to become a Maine Bar member. I spent the hours before the ceremony getting the final VA ID I needed and drove home to Freedom — a small town of only 700 people — to pick up my grandmother. She will be discussed more later, but for now suffice it to say up until the day she died she was my fiercest advocate. The day I found out I passed the bar, she said she had been sitting all morning in her living room, clutching her rosary beads and praying that I got a passing score! Of course, she would be seated first and foremost at my swearing-in ceremony. I picked her up first, and she waited in the parking lot of the VA regional office near Augusta, Maine, while I ran in to get my final VA ID card. After that, it was on to the Augusta courthouse. A theme started here and continued throughout my nine months on the road: even when I was home, I was always in motion!

**THIRD WEEK OF JUNE, 2019:** I traveled to Indianapolis, Indiana, where I had one hearing. This hearing was incredibly successful, as I learned in the first week of July that I had gotten the client 100 percent of total benefits possible for his schizophrenia, retroactively effective to 2011. Even though this was my third hearing, it was my first decision.

To get the client to the hearing, however, I drove from Indianapolis to South Bend, 150 miles away, picked up the client, and brought him to Indianapolis for the hearing. I should have planned to arrive in South Bend, drive to Indianapolis, then drive back to South Bend after the hearing. However, I was a bit too eager to book my flights and overlooked this logistical aspect of my trip. It taught me to be painstakingly thorough with my future travel reservations. Clients absorbed the expenses incurred with getting attorneys to their hearings, so any money I wasted was money that came out of the client's pocket.

On the way back down to Indianapolis I drove through the worst rainstorm I had ever driven though. I was nervous driving with a schizophrenic client. He occasionally told the non-existent people behind him to stop talking about him. We made some conversation but mostly resorted to listening to the radio — anything I could do to keep him calm. I had no prior experience with handling people with mental handicaps. Quite frankly, I was afraid I would be liable for any harm that came to him while we traveled together. Nor would I know how to react if he had an acute schizophrenic episode. I was thrilled; however, that I made the effort to make sure he got to his hearing — his long-awaited chance to be heard by the federal government. The time I spent with him in the car was my fault; I erroneously booked my tickets to fly into Indianapolis and not South Bend. Driving 600 miles in a day was wearisome, but as the reader will see, such trips became a hallmark of the kind of effort I would put into many of my road trips over the next nine months.

The day after this hearing I left with two of my best friends for Newport, Rhode Island, for "Law School Bill's" bachelor party. (I refer to this Bill in this way to differentiate between him and one of my other best friends, "College Bill.") These three guys and I were tight law school classmates who developed a solid friendship over the three years of law school. The bachelor party extended through the third weekend of June. I left early, however, on Saturday, June 22, 2019, to go directly to a hearing in Jackson, Mississippi.

The bachelor party was a great reprieve from the heavy travel and a great reason to see friends I hadn't seen in a few weeks. Such opportunities would be few and far between.

**FOURTH WEEK OF JUNE, 2019:** Sunday gave me a free day in the Jackson, Mississippi, area, which I used to drive over to the Vicksburg National Military Park. I walked the whole 16-mile driving route, at the end of which I was thoroughly exhausted yet proud of myself. It was sweltering with a beating sun and some pretty steep inclines, but I did it. Again the thought entered my mind: How did I get so lucky? This would be the first of many trips to the Jackson VA regional office.

Monday was my hearing, after which I flew to a truly exciting, exotic place to which I had never been before: El Paso, Texas. I arrived early on Tuesday morning and had the rest of the day to myself. I immediately saw an opportunity to do something I would learn to relish: hike in the desert. I looked on Google Maps, eagerly scanning the terrain for a well-defined hiking spot, national park, or anything else exotic I could see. I settled on what would become one of my favorite places: the Organ Mountain Range, just east of Las Cruces, New Mexico. I took a moment to reflect on my last few days. A wild bachelor party, long flights, and a hearing, all spread out between no less than four states: Rhode Island, Mississippi, Texas, and New Mexico. This contemplation dominated my thinking as I drove north of El Paso. This was my first experience with desert hiking, and it was truly something else.

I hope the hike is not something I will soon forget. Essentially, the scenery was stereotypical desert, like something you'd see in *Breaking Bad*. Cacti lined the road, little brown lizards darted around, the blue sky was crystal clear, and there was absolutely nothing between me and the horizon except the occasional massive mountain range. I hiked while listening to Springsteen's new western-themed album, *Western Stars*, which came out the day I was sworn in to the Maine Bar. It made for a solemn occasion, where the visual sensory of the desert was complemented by an album designed to invoke the American West. I perched myself on a rock and was able to overlook the incredible valley sprawling before me while listening to *Moonlight Motel*, off the aforementioned album. It brought tears to my eyes. It was such a beautiful place, shockingly exotic, and quite the tease to what I could explore with this job. I couldn't believe I was looking nearly 40 miles in front of me toward the White Sands National Monument, which I visited before heading back to El Paso. I knew someday I would return to this place. I didn't think it would be as soon as next month.

The next day, Wednesday, June 26, 2019, I had my two hearings in El Paso. This was the first time I had two back-to-back cases, and then I left for Columbus, Ohio. I arrived in Columbus not because I had a hearing there, but because that was the nearest airport (with flights that worked for my hectic schedule) to the actual location for my next hearing, Huntington, West Virginia. I arrived in Columbus at 12:30 a.m. on Thursday, June 27. I stumbled from the airport to the adjacent hotel and spent a few hours sleeping before waking early to drive the two and a half hours south to Huntington. Such a harsh travel schedule ended anticlimactically as one of my hearings was cancelled, but this cancelled hearing had a great effect on me.

The cancelled hearing was for a client who suffered from major depressive disorder and anxiety. As such, he was a nervous wreck even before the hearing started. When the VA hearing coordinator came out to the waiting room to tell us his hearing was cancelled, my client almost flew into a panic attack. This client had a friend drive him to Huntington — an incredible 150 miles away from his home — thereby, expending great expense and time in order to arrive early for a hearing which never happened. A hearing, by the way, he had to wait at least three years to have. He was beside himself, and so was I.

The reader has to understand something fundamental about me: I am a very patient person. I do not snap easily. I go with the flow, which is an outlook one must have if traveling on airplanes as much as I did. I pride myself on being logical with my criticism. If a waiter spills a drink on me in a restaurant, I say, "Did you do it on purpose? Of course not, so why should I get mad at you?" *Intent* is of paramount importance to me. This is my normal mindset. Such was *not* my mindset when the hearing coordinator came out to the waiting room to deliver this devastating news. I did not explode at the hearing coordinator; I respectfully, yet forcefully, requested that I speak to the judge assigned to preside over the hearing. Apparently, she was actually available for the hearing but had to decline to have the hearing due to legal jurisdictional issues.

My anger, however, came from the fact that the VA never told my client or my office that the hearing was cancelled. The VA should have called my client days before. I saw the VA as negligent in this matter, making their action inexcusable. Even though this was the case, some fault rested with me. I should have caught this legal issue myself and asked some questions before solidifying this hearing date.

With my client seated beside me, I spoke with the judge. I did not yell, accuse, or be disrespectful. I informed the judge that I thought there was no excuse for the VA to not contact my client or my office about the hearing cancellation and described in detail the kind of expenses both the client, who was already facing financial hardship, and I had to incur to get to Huntington. I knew my office could absorb the cost of a no-show hearing; it was much harder for my client to do so.

The judge's response was noble. She apologized profusely. She affirmed the permissible cause of the cancelled hearing, but she agreed that the VA regional office should have informed the client when the decision was made days before. She did not get defensive or take umbrage at my direct questions. When I got home, I wrote the VA a nice letter to put in the client's file, giving this judge credit for her handling of the issue. A couple months later, the client was awarded 100 percent of possible benefits, retroactive almost a decade — an extraordinary favorable result stemming from other claims he had in the VA system. So he made out OK, but such a result did not absolve the VA of their failed duty to warn the client of his cancelled hearing.

Nor could the client recoup the expenses he incurred in traveling to the hearing location, as I found out later. I was so perturbed by this VA regulation, which states that a claimant absorbs all costs associated with getting to a hearing, that I wrote a short article on the matter, which was published in the December 2019 issue of the *Court of Appeals for Veterans Claims Bar Journal*. In this article I advocated for changing the law around the issue of reimbursement for cancelled hearings when the client had no prior notice of the cancellation. I was thrilled to adopt this article as further advocacy for the disabled veterans' constituency. I felt like I was making my own mark on the system, as well as providing other kinds of support for my clients. I later passed the article on to a staff member of United States Senator Angus King, in whose office I worked during two college internships. So much the better if it could attract the attention of those in power to change the law.

Ultimately, I returned home at the end of June, thoroughly exhausted from the nearly week and a half I was gone and the unusual amount of travel I did in one trip. Including the previous weekend's bachelor party, over the last week of June, I

(1) drove from Maine to Rhode Island with my two law school friends;

(2) flew from Rhode Island to Mississippi;

(3) exhausted myself walking around a 16-mile battlefield loop in sweltering summer heat;

(4) flew from Jackson, Mississippi, to El Paso;

(5) hiked just north of El Paso;

(6) took a red-eye flight from El Paso to Columbus;

(7) drove from Columbus to Huntington; and finally

(8) flew back to Maine.

And of course, as much as I liked to be home, I loved every second of it! Over the succeeding months it became a running joke in my family that no one could really know for sure where I was at any given moment. I would check in from one part of the country, and maybe a few hours later, I'd pop up in an entirely different part.

# JULY 2019

———◆◆———

**FIRST WEEK OF JULY, 2019:** I had no hearings due to the July 4 holiday, which provided me a blissful reprieve with Catherine. I quickly learned to make the best of the time in state. As I no longer had quality time with Catherine, my friends, or family, I jumped at the opportunity — and made the opportunity — to maintain a healthy social life. Interacting with strangers on the road could be fulfilling, but it was not the same as the quality time you get with people you love. This is another reason I was "always on the move" even when I was home. I made sure to put in the effort to see the people I missed the most. Having such an opportunity once a month or less reinforced how much I appreciated these people in my life and made me work so hard to make the best of the time I had with them.

**SECOND WEEK OF JULY, 2019:** Here is an example of how flexible my travel arrangements could be. Instead of flying out to my next hearing in Lincoln, Nebraska, from Portland, Maine, I rented a car and drove to Burlington, Vermont, to visit my best friend, College Bill. From Burlington, I then flew to Lincoln. It was a nice but quick visit; we sat out on his apartment porch and talked until about 11:30 p.m. He enjoyed telling me about his new girlfriend and generally catching up on each other's lives. We further made plans for our Texas-New Mexico road trip, which would be centered around a hearing I had in Waco coming up in late July.

My opportunities to see College Bill numbered only a couple times a year, so I took every chance to see him. Even short visits like this were worth the effort. We became fast friends in college and stayed in touch ever since. You'll hear more about him later.

From Burlington, I flew to Lincoln, Nebraska. I arrived in state and immediately felt bored. I would have no problem believing that there are actually things to do in Lincoln, but nothing that I *like* to do. I love hiking, as the reader may have gathered already. The first thing I do when I fly into a city is figure out how to leave it, preferably in the direction of the nearest hiking trail. I find the peace and quietness of nature quite soothing. Perhaps this is a function of growing up literally in the middle of the woods back in Freedom. Maybe it has something to do with my desire to always be in control of my surroundings. Regardless, I pride myself on the lengths I'll go to in order to "get outside," and escape the hustle and bustle of city life.

Such was my mindset as I got off the plane in Lincoln, looked around me, and saw only a city and flatness! "This won't do," I thought to myself. I had an entire day to kill once I flew into Lincoln. How was I going to make the most of my time there? The answer: skip town and come back for my hearing. But where to go? I pulled up Google Maps, toggled the terrain feature, and got a crazy idea.

Six hours to the west lay Colorado and the Rocky Mountains. This was my chance. For a long time I had wanted to hike in this storied mountain range. On my cross-country road trip, I drove through Colorado on my way to the West Coast, getting a tease of what the mountains could offer. If I put in the effort, I could get a nice road trip through the plains — another aspect of this country I wanted to further explore — hike in the mountains, and be back in Lincoln by Sunday night. What did I have to lose?

So, Saturday afternoon I drove from Lincoln, Nebraska, to Fort Collins, Colorado. As I described to a friend later on, this road trip was "interestingly boring." On the road there was little to see. Rather, flat prairie land extended to the blue horizon. Little towns or clusters of farm buildings dotted the way. Otherwise, there was not much to draw one's attention. But this was the fascinating part! In Maine, trees or hills prevented the kind of horizon seen in the prairie. As one Kansas farmer hyperbolized to me on my cross-country trip, "I get nervous when I can't see 25 miles in front of me." He, like the people here in Nebraska and prairies of northeastern Colorado, would have a tough time in Maine! I was experiencing something I was not used to, and to me that is the great thrill of traveling. I had an open road, my Spotify blasting, and nothing but time until I got to Fort Collins. I arrived in town late on Saturday night, eager to get out in the morning to hike the mountain I selected, the 7,616-foot-tall Greyrock Mountain.

On Sunday morning I hiked majestic, beautiful Greyrock. I could stand at the top of the mountain and see the Pawnee National Grassland in northeast Colorado, then turn around and follow the Rocky Mountain range to snowcapped mountains to the south. I teared up at the mountain top; I couldn't believe I was actually hiking in the Rockies, a dream come true! Two locals at the top reinforced my belief that I had picked the right mountain in the face of my time constraints. I sat at the top of the mountain, allowed myself to relax for a moment, and simply took in the heavenly sights. I didn't want to leave. It was so peaceful and quiet at the top.

I've grown to almost feel most at home when I am at the top of a mountain. There I am divorced from real life, cut off from outside communications. At the top, you can do nothing but take in the sights.

It was this foray into the Rockies that inspired me to vociferously learn about the Lewis and Clark expedition, which explored much of the Pacific Northwest in the early 1800s. While the scale of their exploration was much larger than mine, I feel like our goals were the same: to learn as much as we can about where we were exploring. Sure, I drove across the prairie and mountains in an air-conditioned car, while they had to fight buffalo, grizzly bears, and the elements, but I still felt a special kinship. We had similar *intent*. I started reading a book by Stephen Ambrose about the expedition, and simply devoured every page. My adventurous spirit only grew stronger.

The drive back to Lincoln was six and a half hours, so I left right after my hike. I was exhausted by the hike, but my sense of accomplishment and excitement kept me awake until I arrived back in Lincoln.

*Looking south from Greyrock Mountain. I could have stayed at the top all day.*

My hearing in Nebraska was Monday afternoon, July 8, 2019. This hearing was eye-opening. The only issue in contention was whether the client's lumbar spine degenerative disc disease was "at least as likely as not" caused by his active duty military service. The client, Philip, was a very prideful man. He cried as he told the judge about how his back precludes gainful employment, physical relations with his wife, and daily activities that a man in his 50s shouldn't be precluded from doing. In service he fell off a tank and landed flat on his back. He has had debilitating back pain ever since that 1980s in-service accident. Talking about his disability was tough to do, and it made me reflect on the situations some of these men face.

The fact is that men are socially conditioned to not talk about their feelings or anything that is not deemed to be "manly." Men are supposed to be the bread-winners, physically tough and emotionally unavailable. Thankfully, such attitudes have been liberalized over the past couple decades as society has socially progressed, but such progress is almost irrelevant for many older men — particularly servicemen who are trained to always "act tough" and never complain when something is wrong. Such is the military's toxic masculinity.

This toxic masculinity haunts veterans later in life, when a back pain they never reported or the mental health issues they suppressed come back to affect their everyday lives. I see this in almost all of my clients in one way or another. The issues snowball until one day the veteran cannot take it anymore, or the issues have compounded in a way that never would have happened if they dealt with problems before it was too late.

This unfortunate, anachronistic attitude men have is the reason I recommend one course of action, above all. When people ask me how they can help veterans of our military, my response is just *listen* to them. Give them a supportive ear. Make it clear that venting problems or describing pain is actually one of the most courageous things they could do. If you ask me, outwardly showing weakness is actually demonstrating inner strength. Reaching out for help is hard, and it should not be discouraged. This is one of the most important life lessons I have learned from helping our veterans. Philip should be very proud of himself. It's not easy. There is a reason why a box of tissues is the one constant in the hearing rooms I've used across the country.

On Tuesday morning, I flew from Lincoln to Montgomery, Alabama, where I had a hearing on Wednesday, a free day on Thursday, and a hearing on Friday. After my hearing on Wednesday morning, I spent some time talking to a disabled veteran out in the regional office parking lot. His name was Ed. He was an overweight, elderly African American man with a kind face and gregarious demeanor. He motored his electrical wheelchair right up to me and sought my advice on his case. He knew I was an attorney because of my suit. He obviously had no issue talking with strangers. He spoke slowly, matter-of-factly, and considerately; he was not afraid to tell me how he got to where he was. I talked with him for maybe 20 minutes or so, helped him get his wheelchair in his van, and then got him over to the driver's seat.

Describing Ed as 100 percent physically disabled would not just refer to his level of monetary compensation. He stepped on a landmine in Vietnam in 1969, fought at Hamburger Hill, and was pursuing special monthly compensation for his mobility issues. He used an electric wheelchair to get around and had a specially adapted minivan to hold this chair. He had to drive himself because he had no one to take him to the regional office. His son, an Afghanistan veteran who was service connected for some conditions, had recently died from a heart attack that made him drive off the highway. Such a father-son military connection was striking — both he and his son were devastated by such useless wars.

Ed was a humble man, self-effacing and non-braggadocio, who was just making his way through life taking each day at a time. I felt much sympathy toward him and gave him my business card. I asked him to call the firm, so we could see if there was anything we could do for him. I was not confident we could do anything if he was already rated at 100 percent, but I could not just leave him empty handed in that parking lot. He was thankful and was another prime example of how meaningful this job was. Meeting him and hearing his story is what finally tipped the scales for me in deciding to put in the effort and keep this journal. I want to remember him and his story.

On my free day on Thursday I visited the Chickamauga National Military Park in Georgia, three hours away. I walked the whole driving route. It was cool seeing the battlefield this way; the first time I was there was in 2007. Growing up, my father and I, sometimes accompanied by my brother, would take each summer between 2004 and 2010 to tour battlefields like this. We three were fascinated by history. Beyond that, it made for fun memories and bonding experiences. They are the reason I give donations, in my father's name every Father's Day, to the American Battlefield Trust.

It was certainly an eerie feeling being at the Chickamauga battlefield without my father, but I really wanted to take advantage of my time in the Deep South, where there are plenty of battlefields to visit.

My Friday hearing was unremarkable. The only noteworthy thing was convincing the judge to decide, on the spot, to issue up-to-date VA exams. In my mind, I consider this a noteworthy accomplishment. Normally a judge takes months to issue a decision and will rarely commit to any course of action on the sport. On that Friday, July 12, 2019, I started this journal waiting in the Montgomery, Alabama airport.

The first several weeks of this job made me realize I would rather do nothing else at this particular junction of my life. My contemporaneous summation of my feelings would be a hallmark of my thoughts on the road:

> "The work is so meaningful and the travel aspect unparalleled, and not to mention fits me and my interests perfectly. I've given myself a few years' deadline; I do not want to do this job when I have kids, out of fairness for both Catherine and me. Therefore, I am trying to live it up while I can, taking advantage of every opportunity that comes my way. The one downside of this job, though, is being away from Catherine for these long periods of time. I miss her so greatly and always almost tear up at the thought of coming home to her. She truly is a shining beacon of my life."

**THIRD WEEK OF JULY, 2019:** This week saw me depart for a hastily-scheduled hearing in Los Angeles, California. Jack called me when I was in Alabama and asked me if I would go; he must have felt that I would have a right to say "no" because of the shortness of time and the distance required. But I heartily agreed. I have no desire to explore the major cities of southern California, but my client's interest in having his hearing *far* outweighed my desire to not go. So I kept my bag packed. I was in California for a relatively short time; I flew out on Sunday morning and flew back home Monday afternoon. But the trip was eye opening.

The hearing itself was unremarkable. But the trip reinforced my aversion to massive cities. I felt neutered by the lack of a rental car, like I wasn't in full control of where I *could* go, but even if I had one, it would have been impractical to go out and explore the mountainous area east of Los Angeles. The reasons, and other negatives, are best explained by my Monday morning Lyft driver, Joe, an Italian immigrant.

The reader will have to note that the views expressed by Joe are the views of only one man, one experience, in one time. I'm sure other people rave about Los Angeles. Joe decidedly did not.

Joe spent some time telling me about how he used to be a chef back in Italy, but in America he was considered too "overqualified" to work in an Italian restaurant. He talked about how Italians cook for the pleasure and customer's satisfaction, not for profit, like here. Back in the home country they only use fresh ingredients and truly take pride in their work. But the profit-motive here meant there was no place for him doing such a job in L.A.

Joe and I had about 30 minutes together (to go five miles) in which he described what LA was really like, according to his own experience. His statements were illuminating. They included telling me about the gangs that roamed some of the neighborhoods; the truly horrific traffic in all parts of the city at all times; the incredible housing costs (he described how a two bedroom, one bathroom, boarded up apartment in a bad neighborhood would go for as high as half a million dollars); how crime was rampant and the local police were unable to do anything as gang members would frequently threaten violence against local police and families (necessitating the non-local feds coming in to help with crime reduction); how he would have to wash his car every two days or so, as, after such a time driving around the city, his car would get coated with black pollutants.

I felt really bad for him. He worked hard to get and stay in this country the right way (he expressed disgust at those who come in illegally and commit crimes and otherwise make a bad name for immigrants). He did everything right: got his citizenship papers, studied for his test, tried to make a living for himself driving Uber and Lyft, but he was stuck in this "sinkhole" with no clear way out. He couldn't do what he wanted, cooking, so he tried to get by however he can. Maybe the Promise of America let him down?

Overall, he painted a dismal picture of the city and stated that after his American wife retires, he wanted to leave as quickly as possible. He reinforced my view that I felt like a prisoner in my hotel. Costs and traffic precluded from going anywhere, and I didn't feel like it was safe to walk places.

I have not been back to Los Angeles since. I'll admit it, I hyped up my own anxiety. I isolated myself in my hotel room, terrified to go anywhere. I spent my time in the city in the hotel lobby, watching a baseball game between the Red Sox and Dodgers. During this trip, my adventurous spirit took a back seat to my concerns. I learned my limits and somewhat regret not doing *something* while in the city.

I completed my hearing and immediately left for LAX. There I had a friendly conversation with Max, an estate planner with Wells Fargo. He was a frat-boy-turned-big-banking-executive straight out of central casting. Picture Schmidt from *New Girl*. He posted up next to me outside a restaurant in our LAX terminal. We both went to law school and took the same bar prep class. To his credit, he passed the extraordinarily difficult California bar. He gave me his card, the information on which reinforced my perception of him. He worked on the 52nd floor of the Wells Fargo building on the same boulevard as the federal building. Some big title for a big job for a big company. Don't get me wrong, he was a nice guy, and we enjoyed comparing notes on law school and bar prep. He was maybe a few years older than me (he stated he graduated from college in 2008). He seemed to be the classic big city, young, ambitious, L.A. executive who got into his field to make a name for himself. He didn't want to follow law as that is what his father did. In other words, we came from totally different worlds, and he was essentially the opposite of Joe the Lyft driver. Max was financially successful, confident, going places, and loved living in and being from L.A. Joe was unhappy to be there, wanted to do something else, and couldn't leave, as much as he wanted to. A tale of two cities, for sure.

The day after Los Angeles I had all of a few hours in Maine on Tuesday morning before I left for New Orleans for four days. I thoroughly enjoyed New Orleans and cannot wait to go back! As the reader will see, it's one of the few major cities in which I actually enjoyed spending time.

The first night I was in town, I first went to Pat O'Brien's, a famous piano bar. I learned later that this was the same bar where my paternal grandfather got kicked out in the 1950s, while in the Navy, for getting into a bar fight. As I said, I only learned this fact later, making my selection of this bar spooky. This was where I first had a signature New Orleans alcoholic drink — the Hurricane. My night was off to a great start.

The most memorable part of the trip, however, was when I visited Ticklers Dueling Piano Bar in the French Quarter. I went in at about 5 o'clock or so, and I was the only customer there. The bar had two pianos and a drummer. I quickly became friendly with the piano players, who, like most pianists in piano bars, played classic rock covers. They asked me where I was from, prompting a reply from many people I met on my travels: "Man, you are a *long* way from home!" I soon found myself the recipient of a private concert. I primarily listen to 1970s-1980s classic rock, so I felt right at home in this bar. Such is part of the reason I seek out piano bars in the first place. As an amateur piano player who played a few open mic nights in college, I appreciate the pianists' courage in performing for a live audience.

After we got talking about our mutual musical tastes, one of the pianists invited me up to duet with him on "Thunder Road" by Bruce Springsteen. This was an extraordinarily fun experience. I actually got to play with a drummer, a microphone, and a decent piano! And if I messed up, it wasn't the center of attention; I could collect myself and jump right back in. I followed the chords of the song on an iPad app. I think I sounded OK, even though it was tough to hear myself. But it was so fun to play with a drummer, taking the pressure off me to keep time and rhythm. Even though I was playing for no one except the bartenders and other musicians, it still was a great time. I will forever be thankful to the pianists who were so laid back as to give me a chance.

After this piano bar, I went over to another live music scene, called Fat Catz. It was right down Bourbon Street. This featured a more soulful, R&B cover band; a few lead singers with a saxophone, drums, guitar, keyboards, and back-up singers. This capped off a great first night in the French Quarter, a place that certainly lives up to its reputation as having its own unique, thriving culture. My perception of the Quarter was helped by the fact that I visited on a weeknight, so it wasn't so overcrowded to be overwhelming. Additionally, my perception was that the night clubs and bars played New Orleans-style R&B and such, not the typical club music I might find if I sought out other night clubs popular with my age group. The Quarter differed from the Portland, Maine "Old Port" in this regard, even if the Quarter reminded me of the Old Port in other ways, like proximity to the water, general layout, and cobblestone streets.

The city left a great impression on me, a rarity for sure! Another thing that helped my perception was the food. So good! I tried all the classic New Orleans staples — as recommended by the internet and locals — and found that I liked everything I tried. I particularly liked fried shrimp po' boys, which are essentially fried shrimp sandwiches.

The day after the piano bar I had a free day in New Orleans. So in the morning I went over to the 1815 battlefield where Andrew Jackson repulsed a British invasion of New Orleans. This battlefield was straightforward; the park clearly delineated American lines versus British lines and conceptually was very easy to grasp, considering the straightforwardness of the British assault. In the Lyft on the way to the battlefield, I passed through a blighted, desolate part of New Orleans. The Lyft driver said this was the fallout and continued struggle resulting from Hurricane Katrina. I was too young to contemporaneously appreciate the disaster that hurricane brought to New Orleans, but I had certainly read about it as I grew older and saw footage of people struggling to seek help from rooftops.

After the battlefield, I spent hours at the New Orleans World War II museum, apparently one of the largest such museums in the world and generally considered to be *the* national World War II museum. The museum is located in New Orleans as 92 percent of all military craft in World War II were manufactured by a company that was based in New Orleans. The museum was impressive and almost had *too* much in it. Hundreds of exhibits walked the visitor through the early stages of World War II, American mobilization, and the downfall of Japan. One could easily spend a full day thoroughly going through the exhibits. I was consistently amazed, almost to the point of choking up, at how Americans so fully rallied beside one another to see us through this all-encompassing war. Seemingly, no one was underutilized. Where did that spirit go? I reflected on the current divisions of our country. What would it take to get back that "We're all in this together" spirit, outside of another world war? Day after day the news reveals deep divisions and controversy. Touring this museum, however, everyone who went through could appreciate and agree on how our "greatest generation" saved this world from a horrific dictator and ideology. Standing at exhibits or talking to other visitors, I did not wonder if they were a Trump supporter, a Democrat, or anywhere in between. Rather, we all simply stood in awe of our predecessors, proud to be Americans, and honored to be able to pay tribute to that wonderful generation. I didn't know it at the time, but one of my grandmother's uncles, Joseph Muchie, served in the 313th Infantry Regiment, 79th Army Division, on World War II's European front. I wish I had known that when I was touring this museum. I feel like it would have made the visit much more personal to me.

A major downside to this trip was that I realized the honeymoon was over. Two months of near constant travel had taken its emotional toll on me. For the first time in this job I found myself feeling truly lonely. I can, and do, easily make conversation with strangers, but this interaction is not as fulfilling as being with friends or with Catherine. I severely missed Catherine. It sucked sleeping alone. It sucked not being able to communicate with her in any meaningful way while I was on the road. A quick message or phone call running between airport gates could never make up for missed face-to-face interactions.

This malaise set in during my last night in the city. I didn't feel like exploring. I didn't feel like going into the piano bar. Quite frankly, I just wanted to sulk in my room. I was ready to leave New Orleans after spending a couple days there, and I was further depressed when I realized I wouldn't have any substantial interaction with Catherine until August 1. She worked nights at a hospital, meaning we would barely cross paths when I did find myself home for an appreciative length of time.

The "sadness and euphoria" characteristic of my adventurous spirit was at a low point that last night in New Orleans. Maybe, this was just a byproduct of being so consistently on the road for the past month and a half. I hoped my spirits would rebound once I had my two-week break in early August. I was further saddened by thinking that Catherine missed me as much as I miss her, yet worse. She was home sulking, while I had at least the opportunity for work and adventure to distract me from wallowing in me missing her. I felt bad that she was left home alone, wedding planning or working hard. At least on this trip, I had my upcoming weekend road trip with College Bill to look forward to, the first meaningful interaction I'd have with friends since Law School Bill's bachelor party in late June. But, at the same time, it was sobering to realize that this separation from Catherine would essentially be normal as long as I did this job.

Such is the nature of this job. I knew something like this was coming, and my coworkers have to deal with this solitude, as well, but this didn't make my feelings any less valid. I learned this week that the new attorney Jack had hired abruptly quit, so travel relief would have to wait even longer than planned.

The trip ended on a positive note, however. The hearing went well, and my Lyft driver on the way to the airport was a fun conversationalist. His name was Ali. He was from Lebanon, had a wife and a 4-year-old child with one more on the way, and went through all the proper channels to become an American citizen. He was eminently gregarious, friendly, talkative, inquisitive, and represented himself well. He was 29 years old. He was telling me how he came to America, the land of opportunity, married an American woman, and was just trying to make it for himself — to live modestly while providing for his family. This is something he could not do in Beirut, Lebanon. He wanted to move to California, but his wife's New Orleans connections kept him in that city for now. He wanted to move to California to be a tow truck driver, which for some reason he thought would be exceptionally lucrative. He was a fun guy. I told him all about Maine, and he seemed to take a genuine interest in what Maine had to offer. I gave him my card with personal info on it in case he ever wanted to check out Maine. Like Joe in Los Angeles, he was a shining example of how the Promise of America — with all its faults and divisions you might see in the news — is still a "shining city on a hill." Sometimes, this is tough to remember.

The end of this week, Saturday July 20, was notable because it was the first time in a month I had seen any Maine-based friends. That day I briefly visited my college friends, Jeremy and Innes, in Biddeford; helped Law School Bill with some yard work around his new house in Gorham; and then went back to his house that night to play poker with him and one of my other best friends, Matt Simone. Spending time with them was rehabilitating and heart-warming. It made me further excited about my two weeks in-state in August, when I would have more of an opportunity to reconnect with friends and get a sense of pre-traveling normalcy.

**FOURTH WEEK OF JULY, 2019:** On Sunday I had an 11 ½-hour layover in Washington, DC, heading from Maine to Florida for a few days full of hearings. My 82-year-old grandfather, "Grandad" — the same one who inspired me to get into the veterans' disability field —, lived in Fairfax, Virginia. I, therefore, planned on spending the day with him between flights. I had a nice day with him. I rented a car at Dulles Airport and picked him up at his house around 9 a.m. We went to the First Bull Run battlefield, the site of the first major battle of the Civil War, which coincidentally happened exactly 158 years ago that day. And, it was exactly five years ago this weekend that we went out to the same battlefield while I was living in Washington, DC, during a summer internship.

It was about 95 degrees or so and very muggy, but he was able and willing to walk about .6 miles around the visitor center and adjacent fields. He was recovering from a surgery to fix an old left foot Vietnam war wound, so it was only out of an abundance of caution that he made the final journey from the visitor center to the parking lot in a wheelchair that visitor center staff procured for him.

Spending time with Grandad was important for me. Growing up I had only seen him once or twice a year. However, our relationship grew very close once we started talking regularly on the phone. I called him almost every day while on my 2017–2018 cross-country road trip. He loved following me around on an AAA map. He was thrilled and so proud of me when I started practicing veterans' disability law, and he was eager to learn of all the places I was visiting. He moved around a lot during his 30 years in the Army, so he was familiar with many of the places I went. I highly valued his advice and life lessons he was not afraid to impart. I valued his opinions as they came from a highly rational and logical mind.

After the battlefield we sat at a subway for about two and a half hours, and we talked about a variety of subjects, including my upcoming wedding — which then was slated for June 2020 — his interest in my student loan situation, and other life-event-type things. He was obviously very concerned about my large student loans, the *other* bane of law students.

I visited Grandad on a Sunday. Monday through Wednesday night I was in Florida. I had a hearing in St. Petersburg on Monday, and then I drove the four hours from Florida's Gulf Coast to the East Coast town of West Palm Beach. The drive was not unusual. Palm trees dotted the admittedly beautiful day, but otherwise the drive was monotonous. I was not thrilled to be in Florida. It was hot, muggy, and flat. I had two hearings on that Tuesday, then stuck around until only Wednesday, as my Thursday hearing was cancelled. But at least we had notice of this cancelled hearing.

The grand highlight of this trip was my Wednesday visit to the Kennedy Space Center, two hours north of West Palm Beach. Here was NASA's premier space flight complex and an absolutely jaw dropping interactive museum, primarily dedicated to telling the story of NASA 1960–present. They had focused exhibits on the Apollo program, the Space Shuttle program, the International Space Station, the recent Mars missions, and NASA's current shift toward private partnership with Boeing and Space X.

Some of these exhibits were very moving. Particularly noteworthy was the garden tribute to all the Apollo missions; the elaborate exhibition on the Atlantis, the last space shuttle to fly (in 2011 — I remember watching its launch); and the tour of the Apollo 11 complex a short 15-minute drive from the main Kennedy Space Center Visitor Center. The "lunar theater," a dramatic retelling of the final minutes before Apollo 11 landed on the moon, was also inspiring and made me tear up. Like when I visited the New Orleans-based World War II museum, I was floored by how, for one moment, the American people banded together in a common struggle. Here it was, the American focus on getting man on the moon before the Russians and in time for President Kennedy's 1969 deadline. It was also moving to see original film clips of people all over the world watching the moon landing as it happened — for a moment the world was held captive by their shared encouragement of those three brave men in the Apollo 11 spacecraft. This shared spirit was also captured by newspaper displays around the Apollo visitor center complex, showing world reactions to men first setting foot on the moon. Maybe, a similar spirit will take over us when we set foot on Mars. Seeing these exhibits and the breathtaking accomplishments, I remember thinking, "Man, I am doing nothing with my life." Obviously this was not true, but the thought serves as a testament to how well the visitor center portrayed the accomplishments of the thousands of engineers, pilots, astronauts, and others associated with NASA. If only we could redouble our efforts toward scientific discovery, like we did in the 1960s, the world might be a much more inspiring place.

I left the Kennedy Space Complex highly satisfied with my visit. I was there for a good four or five hours, and I certainly felt like I got my money's worth. I was there in 2007 — when my folks went to Disney World — but I do not remember anything except the Astronaut Training Experience. Since then, the complex has added, at least, the Atlantis shuttle (it was so cool to see the shuttle up close), as that last mission happened four years after our Disney World trip. It provoked chills when, in the Atlantis part of the complex, the theater voiceover stated "Welcome Home, Atlantis," as uplifting fanfare blasted out from speakers, and the wall dramatically lifted to reveal the suspended shuttle "in flight." Also new were the Mars rover missions, NASA/Boeing/SpaceX partnerships, and certainly the more technologically advanced exhibits. Therefore, I was essentially going for the first time. This was certainly a much better use of my time than just aimlessly wandering around West Palm Beach.

Maybe because of my disinterest in Florida, the ever-present loneliness I first felt in New Orleans presented itself here. I opined to Catherine later that being in these unexciting places leads me to only think about how I miss her, my friends, and my family. If I were in a place I was excited about, like the Rocky Mountains or the desert, I would have more to focus on than my loneliness. I think this theory rang true when I was in Nebraska and would otherwise be reinforced by the fact that the loneliness only crept up on me when visiting the flat, hot South, at least the portions that were far away from any battlefield. (Even though New Orleans was interesting, maybe I first felt the loneliness there because I was there for so long and was experiencing a new culture that I would have enjoyed learning about with someone else.)

As my Thursday hearing was cancelled, I returned home Wednesday night. I was glad to spend an extra 24 hours in Maine with Catherine. On Friday, July 26, 2019, I left for Texas for my pre-hearing road trip with College Bill.

## END OF THIRD WEEK, FIRST HALF OF FOURTH WEEK OF JULY, 2019:

On Friday I left in the afternoon for Dallas, Texas. There I was supposed to meet College Bill. We planned this road trip to continue an annual road-trip tradition we started in 2018. That year, we drove around the Gaspé Peninsula of Quebec, Canada. This year, 2019, we wanted to plan a trip but had to do it around my work schedule. As we started planning the trip and figuring out where we wanted to go, I saw that I had a hearing scheduled in Waco, Texas, on Monday, July 29, 2019. The wheels got turning and smoke came out of my ears. Bill and I brainstormed hard to figure out how we could explore the desert and still get to my Monday hearing on time.

The plan was this: On Friday, Bill would fly from Burlington, Vermont (where he lived), to Dallas, Texas. I would fly from Portland, Maine, to Dallas. We would meet in Dallas, rent a car, and that weekend drive all around Texas, southeastern New Mexico, back into Texas, and arrive in

Waco in time for my Monday hearing. Perfect! We would have a nice 1,500-mile road trip, with hiking opportunities along the way and some quality time together.

I was nervous that I wasn't going to make my flights and connectors, but evidently the timeliness of the flights and ease of getting down to Dallas was a precursor to how fun our three-and-a-half-day road trip would be.

Bill spent the late morning and early afternoon in Dallas as he waited for me to arrive. I arrived at about 5:30 p.m. local time and made my way to the rental car center. We decided to drive about four and a half hours to Lubbock, Texas — far more than we anticipated going Friday night — but this allowed us to spend more time hiking and doing other things over the course of the trip. Characteristically, this car ride was classic "us": constant conversation, blasting the mellow classic rock Sirius XM station The Bridge, and laughing interspersed with moments of heavy conversation, maybe about our family, jobs, or any of the other countless subjects on which we could speak more frankly than with anyone else. On the way to Lubbock we saw sprawling wind turbine farms, oil fields, and flatness. We arrived in Lubbock around 10:30 p.m. and decided to go to bed in preparation of an early start Saturday morning

On Saturday we drove from Lubbock, Texas to Las Cruces, New Mexico, via Roswell, New Mexico, the Mescalero Indian Reservation, Alamogordo, New Mexico, and a hike through the Organ Mountain Range.

Roswell was interesting. It's a small town, and we didn't stop to see what kind of attractions they had, but it was still cool to say we drove through the town where conspiracy theorists assert residents encountered a 1947 UFO crash, thereby meeting aliens for the first time under the government excuse of watching a "weather balloon" explosion. We captured a picture of a UFO museum but did not go inside.

The Mescalero Apache Indian reservation was where we wanted to go hiking, but we could not find an adequate spot. The reservation seemed much like a drier Maine — still full of trees and otherwise not desolate, like the surrounding plains and desert. We worked our way from potential hiking spot to spot until we gave up and just continued to the Organ Mountain Range, which the reader may recall I visited in June.

We stopped for lunch in a fantastic sandwich shop in Alamogordo, New Mexico, one of the last towns before hitting the San Andres Mountain range. This town was awesome. The skyline was punctuated by the imposing San Andres mountain range, and it was with regret we learned the range and surrounding wildlife refuge was closed to the public due to its proximity to the White Sands Missile Testing Range. Excitedly, while looking at the town's Wikipedia page we saw a magnificent vista of the towns and surrounding mountains from the top of Thunder Road. I quickly impressed upon Bill my love for the Bruce Springsteen song of the same name — something else the reader may recall from my entry on Ticklers Dueling Piano Bar in New Orleans. So we drove to the top of Thunder Road to get a picture like the one we saw online. The view was magnificent. My growing love of the southwestern desert was only reinforced by sweeping vistas like this.

It's not often people can say they have literally made a dream come true, but that's what happened when Bill and I went to the Organ Mountain Range. But I neglected to mention in my June entry that some months before my visit I had a dream that went like this: I was perched on a rock ledge overlooking a magnificent valley. Even though I could not see him, I had the feeling that Bill was right next to me. We were camping at a site dotted with other tents. That's it. Nothing spectacular. However, I was moved to shocked awe in June when I visited the Organ Mountains and realized that that hike was exactly the valley view I had seen in my dream. It was all so very clear. I then hoped that someday Bill and I would come to this same mountain range — I felt like it was either destiny or written in stone some other way. I would have disbelieved anyone who said to me in that fourth week of June 2019 that in the fourth week of July 2019, I would make the dream come true. But sure enough, Bill and I rolled into the valley and quickly started to hike the four-mile loop first recommended to me by the park's visitor center staff. I told Bill about my dream before we arrived at the mountain range, and he was moved to share this experience with me. We hustled up the trail because we were antsy from sitting all day. At the top of the ridge we stopped to take in the view. For orientation, we posted up on a rock, facing east toward the White Sands complex and the town of White Sands. It was another clear day with barely a cloud in the sky. When we stopped, I asked Bill if he would indulge me and listen to *Moonlight Motel*, the same Springsteen song I listened to, to punctuate my visit a month ago and the song to which I will forever have an association with this particular mountain range. We listened in silence. Bill agreed the appropriateness of the song was fantastic. And there, sitting on the rock overlooking the mountain range with my best friend, I made a dream come true. My affinity for this particular place exponentially grew.

We continued the next half hour or so to Las Cruces, content on lodging there for the night.

The next day, Sunday, July 28, 2019, we drove from Las Cruces, New Mexico to Abilene, Texas. On this route we drove through western Texas and hiked Guadalupe Peak in the Guadalupe National Park, about an hour east of El Paso.

The route between El Paso and Abilene was unexpected in so far as this kind of geography was *exactly* what we were looking for when planning this road trip. Desert stretched out before us into the horizon! In some parts only two colors would dominate the view around us: the brownish desert and the blue sky. We could see that far! Imagine a piece of paper evenly divided into two rectangles by a horizontal line. The top is blue and the bottom is brownish/green/shrubby. That is what it was like driving along this route through western Texas. We took many pictures and marveled at how barren the place was. The flatness was only interrupted by imposing mountain vistas, standing like immovable sentries over this undefiled nature. This is what I love about the desert. It is wide open and not as crowded as the East Coast or any given city, but when it is not flat, it is because of a tall mountain or mountain range, just waiting to be hiked. Overall the region was serene. I wanted to go back, drive a couple miles off the main highway, and simply revel in the absolute peace. We passed large cattle ranches, fenced pens for cows, and dilapidated buildings obviously disregarded years ago. It was simply otherworldly.

I didn't think anything we would see on this trip would overshadow the view from the Organ Mountains, but this national park did in spades. Bill and I hiked Guadalupe Peak, 8,600 feet high, with at least 3,000 feet of elevation gain, in an hour and 34 minutes. The view from the top was breathtaking, making everything below seem almost fake or like computer generated imagery. We were overlooking the Chihuahua Desert and could see, according to one local at the summit, 60 to 100 miles in front of us. After we got a picture at the top and had water and snacks, we started down, breaking into a trail run for the last half of the way down. By the end, we were exhausted but proud of ourselves. The sun was beating down and temperatures got up to 100 degrees; this added to the physical intensity of this magnificent hike.

After we got back to the car, we continued on to Abilene, where we lodged for the night. We arrived around 10:30 and did not go out. I don't think our legs allowed us to move!

On Monday, July 29, 2019, we traveled from Abilene to Waco, where I had to arrive around 11:30, for a hearing that started at 12:30. This hearing went more smoothly than any other hearing I had yet done. I arrived at the regional office around 11:15, went to the bathroom, and connected with my client. She was a sweet, 75-year-old widow who was fighting for the VA's recognition that her husband was heavily exposed to asbestos in service, which thereafter caused his hideously prolonged death years later. We were immediately taken into the hearing room, a full 45 minutes before the hearing was slated to start. The judge was very sympathetic to my client, and I think I did a good job of soliciting testimony on the one issue on appeal. Just as quickly as I came in, I left. The whole hearing lasted 20 minutes.

We proceeded the hour and a half to Dallas, stopping along the way at The Czech Stop, a Czech-centric pastry and sandwich shop. This would not have normally been the kind of place Bill and I would seek out to eat, but we wanted to try it based on a recommendation. The various pastries and dishes reminded me of all the Eastern European sweets my grandmother would make. We walked in, and I said to Bill, tongue-in-cheekily, "This is why Grandma had her heart attack."

We rolled into Dallas around 3 p.m. and searched for something to do before heading downtown (called Deep Ellum) for dinner. We realized that Dealey Plaza, where President Kennedy was assassinated, was less than a mile from our hotel. We therefore headed in that direction, and I think both of us were more moved by visiting the assassination site than we originally thought. We watched the Zapruder film while standing on the grassy knoll, easily able to piece together what happened. Two x's on the pavement marked the spots where JFK was shot, once in the back and once in the head. We never realized that Kennedy was basically at the end of his parade route when he was shot. A couple hundred more yards and he would have been clear of surrounding buildings.

We headed back to the hotel to figure out where to go out for the night. We decided on a restaurant called St. Pete's Dancing Marlin, where we indulged in many mixed drinks and excellent fish tacos. Whenever I would want to go out in town, I immediately looked to Google to find the best-rated place around. St. Pete's was it.

Here we met Gino, our waiter, who presented an inspiring life story. He told us how he left his small-town Michigan home in his early 20s, seeking to not fall into the trap of never leaving his hometown like many of his high school friends. He only told his mother he was leaving after he left the state. He didn't even pack any possessions — he arrived in Dallas with only a small pack and "started walking," looking for job opportunities and a living situation. He settled on various waiting jobs and now has a wife and kid, having made a modest living and finding what he cast out for: independence and a sense of self. His decisions were self-reinforcing by visits home where he would see his high school friends stuck in the same jobs and going nowhere. When we left, he said we were the kind of customers who make his job, who are fun to talk to and make the social part of his job worth it. Over the course of this dinner I told Bill about my desire to write lyrics inspired by people I met and places I visited while in this traveling job. Maybe I would have enough lyrics to ask someone to write music to them. I said I loved the idea of the cover art being the picture I took of a sunrise through the driver's side mirror and the title being the double-meaning *Looking Back*. While I ultimately did not select that title for the book, that picture is what you see on the cover.

Stories like Gino's inspired me to try my hand at creative writing. I would write these poems or lyrics in my yellow legal pad, usually on one of the typical late-night airplane rides home or waiting at an airport gate. I would draw a line down the page. On the left side would be the "tell me" column, and the right side would be "show me." I would start by writing out in the "tell column" the facts of what I wanted to write about. This gave me a template to then get more creative in the right hand "show me" column. This is what I wrote in "show me" column:

> *The sun came up, no one was awake*
> *except Gino tempting faith.*
> *He packed a bag and sold the rest,*
> *said "hey buddy, I'm going west."*
>
> *He hopped on a plane, no second guess;*
> *Folks didn't know his restlessness,*
> *And when he got to Dallas,*
> *He settled and made his palace.*
> *He needed a place and steady pay,*
> *So he made his way to Deep Ellum's gates.*
>
> *Ten years on he had a kid, Found a darlin'*
> *He's waiting tables, at Saint Pete's Dancing Marlin.*

Back to the trip. We checked out a couple more bars before heading over to Louie Louie's Dueling Piano Bar, an establishment we spotted while canvassing Deep Ellum, but they did not open until 9 p.m. Monday nights featured a nine-piece blues band jam session. We were there from 9 p.m. until 12 or so — really late for me! This band, quite frankly, was one of the best live concert experiences Bill or I have ever seen. The band was so tight, a wall of sound executed with superior professionalism. They played Motown/soul/blues covers, my favorites being "She Caught the Katy" and "Signed, Sealed, Delivered." Bill and I were consistently blown away, frequently turning to each other with our jaws agape in response to what we were hearing and seeing. I don't think a smile left my face over the entire three hours we were there. We couldn't believe we were seeing this for free, and that there were so few people in the bar. The horns were powerful, piano, bass, vocals, everything! Just so good. The band was called Elm Street Blues, and they were a collection of professional musicians who got together every Monday night at this bar and jammed to their favorite songs. I was very jealous. We were told they were working on their first extended play, and Bill and I both agreed we needed to keep an eye out for when it was released. As it turns out, as I was refining this part of my book for publication, I opened Spotify to see if their music had yet been released. Sure enough, as of July 3, 2020, they had three songs on Spotify. Definitely look them up.

In a display of his never-ending affection for my generosity in paying for most of this trip, Bill surprised me and bought me a shirt from the bar. I was moved by this, and he gave me two different hugs when he gave it to me. His never-ending gratitude was reinforcing and left me satisfied that he appreciated the opportunity this trip afforded both of us.

On Tuesday, July 30, 2019, we slept in until about 8 a.m. We had a few hours to kill before we had to get to the airport, so we fulfilled a tertiary goal of ours, previously cast aside when we decided the night of the 26th to go to Lubbock and not Amarillo. We dashed into Oklahoma, as neither of us had been there before. We got as far as Marietta, about half an hour or less from the Texas/Oklahoma border. It was a short venture, a three-hour round trip made purely for bragging rights and a sense of doing something worthwhile with our time before this trip ended. We had a happy goodbye at gate E16 of the Dallas-Fort Worth International Airport, immensely thankful for our time together over the past few days.

My overall reflections closely mirror those of our July 2018 Canada trip. This part of this journal entry was written on August 13, 2019. I wanted to give myself a couple weeks to reflect on the trip. I cherish Bill as a friend and can think of no one else with whom I would rather take a road trip. We gelled perfectly — nothing ever bothered us; we put up with and actively encouraged each other's silliness; we enjoyed the same musical choices; and importantly, we both sought to challenge ourselves wherever we decided to ditch the car and explore the desert. I am assured by the sense that he was looking forward to this trip as much as I was, and his text message to me after the trip, "Dude, I gotta say, that was an INCREDIBLE trip. I could not have asked for a better time. Glad to have shared it with you," reinforced my belief and desire that he appreciated our time together as much as I did. It's not easy to put up with someone for literally 24 hours a day for a few consecutive days, but we did and would have done more if we could have. We truly are "Lewis and Clark." Near the end of the trip we talked about what a third annual trip would look like, mutually acknowledging our shared excitement for the possibility of a Pacific Northwest trip. The Lewis and Clerk parallels roll on . . .

We both immensely enjoyed where we went as well. We were especially awestruck by West Texas leading into Guadelupe National Park and our drive through New Mexico. In this way, we certainly achieved our primary goal.

However, this trip took on a different character than our 2018 Canada trip. The Canada trip began three of the best weeks of my life. I was coming off grueling bar study, confident that I had passed, and gleeful to be done with my 20 years of continuous schooling. The trip to Canada allowed me to disconnect from my Portland-centric life for a little bit, take a breather from the hardest academic experience I had ever endured, and allowed me to reconnect with non-law school friends. I felt like I could truly let loose and relax and not feel guilty about doing so. Relax, that is, without the constant pressure or reminder that I could be studying, the same affliction suffered by law students while studying for the Bar.

This Texas trip, on the other hand, was the last leg of almost two nearly constant months of traveling. Fun traveling, don't get me wrong, but heavy travel nonetheless. The Texas trip was also the first time I had experienced my fun traveling with others. Like I told Bill, traveling gets very lonely, so it was even more fun when I could share it with someone who also could truly appreciate the novelty of our shared experiences.

Overall, one could obviously see our trip was time I will cherish forever, and the opportunity to take him on such a trip is something I would do again in a heartbeat.

*Classic desert. Brownish-green grass or dirt until the horizon, unless a silent sentinel — a constant travel companion — stands in the way.*

*The top of Guadalupe Peak. Ever-competitive College Bill, left, pushed us to get to the top as quickly as possible to beat his girlfriend's ex-boyfriend's ascent time.*

*Looking out across the vast, motionless desert. We were so high up that everything looked computer generated.*

*A panorama College Bill took at the Organ Mountains National Monument, me at left. Rarely have I been more at peace than sitting on those rocks, looking out toward White Sands.*

# AUGUST 2019

——— ◆ ———

**SECOND WEEK OF AUGUST, 2019:** This week of travel started on the Tuesday, with an entirely unremarkable trip to Pittsburgh. An East Coast city — how boring! By now I was of the mindset that if I was to travel for work, I really wanted to go to novel places. Also by now, I was ready to get back to the desert.

My client was the most interesting part of the trip; he was a veteran in his mid-50s and seemed like a really fun, down-to-earth guy. You couldn't tell he had a hard time dealing with several horrible memories of his time in service. I flew into Pittsburgh in the afternoon, had the hearing Wednesday morning, and flew home Wednesday night. I had no grand desire to explore Pittsburgh, and I knew I would be down there again in early September. My short travel break was off to a slow start.

On Friday, my twin brother, Kyle, my father, Chuck, and I drove down to Gettysburg, Pennsylvania, for a weekend trip. My dad and I were last there in 2017, and this was the first trip the three of us took since going to Florida to see Billy Joel in 2014. This visit, which we calculated to be my 13th, was the first time we biked around the battlefield. This was much more fun than driving or walking, and it afforded great exercise while expeditiously viewing the entire national park.

Despite my repeated visits to the battlefield, this was the first time I went looking through the prism of my work. I had read all about the battle growing up. (I took an obsessive interest in American history when I was young. I could name all the presidents in order when I was 8 years old.) I read about the political implications of the war, the different battles, leaders, and consequences. However, this was the first time I considered the post-battle human cost — the survivors who lived with injuries incurred during their military service. I wondered if there were any 1860s lawyers who devoted their careers to helping disabled veterans. Certainly not in the form I do now, as the idea of the Department of Veterans Affairs or any other recourse veterans had for redress from their government did not start until after the Civil War.

Civil War-era veterans did not know about PTSD, access to medical technology that makes living with disabilities easier, or the numerous resources available to today's veterans, like vocational rehabilitation training. As hard as disabled veterans have it now, I can't imagine what veterans of past conflicts had to endure. As frustrating and inefficient as the VA can be, we have to be lucky that there is a whole bureaucracy dedicated to helping veterans in the first place! The VA is a victim of its own size, for sure, but the people who work there and across the country do, truly, have the best interest of veterans in mind. VA employees carry out the veteran-friendly policies and rules enacted by the executive and legislative branch. What they do is supremely important. Next time you see one, thank them.

**THIRD WEEK OF AUGUST, 2019:** On Sunday, Kyle and Dad dropped me off in Philadelphia, where I had a hearing on Monday. I took the day to visit the Liberty Bell, Independence Hall, and walk around Philadelphia's historic block. The reader can see my affinity for American history is never-ending.

This Monday hearing concerned one of my most memorable clients, Peter. Peter is a Navy veteran who is a fighter, salt of the earth, and entirely devoted to his family's well-being. Peter served for four years in the active duty Navy on assignments where he was exposed to radiation daily. This radiation is now what has caused his terminal colon cancer, and his cancer is the condition for which we were seeking "service connection" — VA recognition that the problem is "at least as likely as not" due to his military service. I knew right from our first conference call that this was a different client. He is a natural conversationalist; was as interested in getting to know me as I was to know him; and was obviously fighting this service connection on principle. He asserted he didn't care about the money, he just wanted the government to recognize that they caused his current cancer, which he had been fighting for the past five years. He loved his time in the Navy and would do it all again, but the daily exposure finally caught up to him. This was the first time that a client suggested that he and I meet before the hearing. He and his wife, Linda, wanted to take me out to dinner and get to know me the night before the hearing. I heartily agreed. We went to a place in Philadelphia called The Black Taxi, a nice little Irish pub. Despite my intense lobbying, Peter picked up the tab. He said I should use the firm's money "on the next client." We sat there for close to two hours. We debriefed more thoroughly on Peter's case, and I told him about my job and my travels.

My job felt more heavy than ever; Peter's case sparked a short-lived crisis of confidence. This was the last great struggle of his life — fighting for the injustice that was the VA not recognizing the damage the Navy did to him (with the VA's previous denial of benefits relying on the worst medical examination I'd ever read). It was up to me to prove his case and make the years-long struggle worth it. The realization of this weight almost moved me to tears and convinced me to hustle back to my hotel room that night and do another pass on Peter's file before the hearing the next morning. Now more than ever I wanted to make sure I did as thorough a job as possible, concisely and clearly conveying to the judge the evidence in favor of Peter's argument; detailing the copious radiation exposure Peter incurred in service; and proving that he was indeed suffering from colon cancer and several other secondary conditions as a result of either the cancer itself or the chemotherapy. Honestly, I unexpectedly felt overwhelmed by the weight. He was relying on me to do all this, like all clients do. But meeting Peter not only put a face to the case — something that happens for all my hearings — but he provided me a story — a situation, a challenge — and rested his last hopes on me (even though I conveyed to him that no matter what happens, this was not the end of the road). Like his cancer, Peter was going to fight the VA until he won or died trying to win. But for sure, he was not going to give up. So I wasn't going to give up either.

Peter and I were the first to arrive at the VA regional office the next morning. He sympathetically testified to the judge. Remarkably, Peter still loved the Navy and was moved to tears when talking about how he has only recently been forced to be medically discharged due to his chemotherapy, and would do everything all over again. His devotion to his country and to other people was inspiring. He choked up telling the judge about a situation off the coast of Libya where he had to arm the ship's nuclear weapons. To Peter it was real life, but it really was just a drill. He refused to let any other shipmate be the one to arm, and if necessary, fire the missiles. He thought that he did not want that action on anyone else's conscience. He thought he would start World War III if he fired those missiles; he didn't want anyone else to live with that guilt. He said he voluntarily signed up for the Navy during the Gulf War. He said, "There was a war going on, and I wasn't going to miss out." Such is his character.

Later on I wrote a poem — the kind of which the inspiration was so clear the words just flew out of the pen. I simply called it "Peter's Song."

*He was born on the streets of Philly.*
*Peter served his time in the Navy.*
*He recalls his time with a grin,*
*even though the cancer's closing in.*
*You see, get too close to those damn machines,*
*they'll fry your body like you've never seen.*

*So Peter gets out of bed, goes to fight*
*For life, wife, and justice for his kind.*
*He didn't ask for this to happen, but he would do it again*
*Because Peter, you wish you knew, was just that kind of man.*

*Back in the '80s, there came a time*
*the missiles were primed, and Peter might need to send men to die.*
*His hands trembled, his body was tense,*
*But no way this would fall on his friends' consciousness.*
*He didn't ask for this to happen, but would do it again*
*Because Peter, you wish you knew, was just that kind of man.*

*His eyes glisten, he chokes back tears*
*Five kinds of chemo fill you with five kinds of fear,*
*But he soldiers on, like soldiers will*
*And tells the judge about his many ills.*
*He didn't ask for this to happen, but he would do it again*
*Because Peter, you wish you knew, was just that kind of man.*

Anticlimactically, the hearing went exactly as any other hearing would. At the end of the hearing I was satisfied with the information we put on the record, knowing that anything that was marginalized or inadvertently left off the record would be included in my post-hearing memo to the judge. Such was the unusual nature of an administrative tribunal like the Board of Veterans' Appeals. Unlike courts of law, a board hearing does not have to abide by any rules of evidence or courtroom procedure. In short, I could say or submit anything of relevance to a client's case. This kind of system is highly favorable to veterans, as it gives them every opportunity to prove their cases.

However, at the time of this writing, this story does not have a happy ending. The judge rendered her decision in November and denied each and every claim. She assigned much probative value to the VA's own medical examination of Peter. I was infuriated and disappointed when I learned of this decision. I emailed Jack, my boss, with the six major reasons why I thought the VA exam was inadequate and wondered aloud how the judge could have possibly relied on it. It's like the judge didn't even listen during the hearing, or read my post-hearing memo to her! Such reliance on a shoddy exam was mind boggling, but it also provided a sound basis to appeal the judge's decision to the Court of Appeals for Veterans Claims. At the time of this writing the Court of Appeals had remanded Peter's case (erasing the board judge's denial), starting the process over again.

I felt I had to deliver the bad news to Peter myself. As a matter of course, Jackson and MacNichol sends a letter to clients when we get a board decision, telling them what the judge decided and what we think of the result. However, when the decision is really unexpected — either in a good way or bad way — I prefer to call my clients to deliver the news. Peter's case was one of the few where I had only bad news to deliver. Peter could tell I felt awful, and he tried to comfort me. "You're right," he said. "I got the sense the judge wasn't listening either; we did all we could." I expected no other reaction. This is the guy who comforted his doctor when the doctor tearfully admitted that he misdiagnosed Peter's cancer, allowing the cancer to progress far after it was too late to effectively treat.

Back to the hearing. I rushed out of the regional office, a quick handshake and goodbye to both Linda and Peter, jumped in a Lyft, and drove over to the airport. I arrived with a mere 10-minute cushion before my plane boarded. My next destination would turn out to be my most favorite of all my travels.

I was assigned to an August 20, 2019, hearing in Sheridan, Wyoming. However, a quick look at the map revealed that there was really no easy way to get to Sheridan from any major airport. Perfect! That characteristic smoke started coming out of my ears. I had the opportunity to make a considerable road trip out of this Wyoming assignment. I had been itching to get out to the Rocky Mountains again after my short foray to Fort Collins, Colorado. I had heard wonderful things about Wyoming from my parents, who visited out there while my mother was in law school. Furthermore, the chance to get out to Wyoming for work was probably very rare. Jackson and MacNichol has clients all over the country, but understandably the clients are primarily where the population is — big cities, the East and West Coast, and relatively few in the "fly over" states. Wyoming is the least populated states in the country, and there were three other traveling attorneys to share the hearing load. Therefore, I recognized from the beginning that this was one trip I probably would never again get to do for work. I had one day between Peter's hearing in Philadelphia and the hearing in Sheridan. I had a further day after the Sheridan hearing until I had to fly home. How would I make the most of this trip?

The planning came together easily. On August 19, I flew into Denver — the gateway to the Rockies — and immediately felt that adventurous spirit return to me, the one that refused to rally given my recent East Coast city hearings. I jumped in the rental car, got on the highway in Denver, blasted

Bob Seger's "Roll Me Away," and knew right then I was in for a treat. My GPS said 376 miles to Sheridan, Wyoming. It was a straight shot up from Denver. The initial part of the drive doesn't compare to what I would later see. Southeastern Wyoming is relatively like its border with Colorado: plains, flat, not very mountainous. I did, however, see a magnificent sunset and drove until 9:30 p.m., at which point I arrived at my hotel in Sheridan.

On August 20, I arose early and had a great hearing. The judge was extremely thorough, a true friend to the claimant, and heavily implied he was going to grant "total disability" back to March 2015. This is the most favorable scenario for a veteran, where they are paid about $3,100 a month, tax free, for as long as they are unemployable because of their service-connected disabilities. The judge was so thorough as to base his favorable decision on an important, little known legal technicality called "the bilateral extremity factor," which states that the rating for a veteran's extremities can be increased based on disability of the opposite extremity. This judge did his homework.

The reader may ask why the judge was not impartial. Wasn't the role of a veteran's advocate left to me? If the judge was actively looking out for the client's best interest, why was I there? There is some truth to this suspicion. In the veterans' disability system, judges have a legal responsibility to grant benefits wherever possible. In this way, Board of Veterans' Appeals judges are far different from the kind of judges you see in a typical courtroom. In a sense, they are empowered to be advocates. My role as the attorney is almost complementary to such a pro-claimant judge. That said, an advocate like myself was expected to be far more prepared than a judge might, as a judge might hear six or seven other cases that day. While the judge had power to grant benefits, my job was to make sure the judge knew how exactly he could grant benefits. Sometimes the path to "granted" wasn't always clear.

In this case, my client was actually fairly young at only 42 years old. We argued that his service-incurred major depressive disorder not only precluded gainful employability, but any semblance of a social life. This latter part led him to Wyoming in the first place. Fed up with cities, he absconded to Wyoming's ruralness, where many counties have less than one resident per square mile. He lived on a mountain top, in almost total isolation. I could relate to this — I had a strong and growing desire to live on the same ridge in Freedom where I grew up. We talked about how much we enjoyed nature's peace and serenity.

Luckily, the hearing started on time and ended after about 45 minutes. I got out of the regional office at around 10 a.m., ready to go tackle the mountain I had selected to hike, the 3.4-mile trail leading to the Black Mountain Lookout, in the adjacent Bighorn National Forest. My goal, like my goal for every road trip, is to never drive the same route twice. Therefore, I had to take a different route to get back to Denver by the next day. This different return route took me in a slightly hooked path down the center of Wyoming, straight through the Bighorn National Forest.

How do I describe what I saw that day, August 20, 2019, starting with this hike and proceeding until I finished the day in Riverton, four hours south? When I wrote this journal entry on August 21, I felt like I did not possess the vocabulary to adequately describe the immense imagery I saw that day. If someone asked me to imagine the most beautiful landscape I would ever see, I don't think I would come close to describing this particular tract of Wyoming. But I will attempt to have my words do it justice.

The hike itself was almost un-notable. It was essentially a challenging nature hike, through wooded areas similar to what I would find in Maine. But the destination had importance and should have conveyed to me the view I would see. The "lookout" was a structure occupied during the heavy wildfire seasons, so an observer could spot an early stage forest fire and call for support in a reasonable amount of time. Therefore, the observation point, the summit of Black Mountain, was entirely clear-cut; in fact it is situated on top of a rock scramble and had a commanding, 360-degree view of the Bighorn National Forest. Its elevation was 9,500 feet, making it by far the tallest mountain I had ever hiked (but with only one thousand feet of elevation gain). It was fairly windy, but not prohibitive of me capturing video and pictures. I sat for about 20 minutes on the edge of a rock and talked with a fellow hiker. His name was Kaiden, and he was hiking with his dog, Ripley. He was from Montana, 19 years old, and not sure what he wanted to do in life. He was a barista in a Billings, Montana coffee shop. He wanted to travel and explore, maybe be a jack of all trades. The world was certainly his oyster.

We both were stricken by the view. From the top, I could see what looked like a plateau-type shelf extending from this already clearly delineated forest "shelf," on which sat what looked like a massive plain! Let me try to describe it another way: picture a flat ground level, but then a massive, 8,000-foot plateau (not mountain, but long, flat plateau), which you can clearly delineate from the ground level. And then from that elevated plateau, a part that juts out, on which this plain sat. Thus was the sheer vastness of this area. It was all so clear, not only in terms of geography, but the colors that filled in the landscape. Sharp, green trees impressed upon a clear blue sky. It was simply magical. I messaged pictures to the family group, and said, "I don't want to leave." I sat there for a while, longer than I intended, even after Kaiden and Ripley departed. At that moment, I truly did not want to leave.

*Looking out over the Bighorn National Forest. Wyoming is a mystery wrapped in an enigma. I can't wait to go back.*

Eventually though, I had to, so I made my way back to the car and continued west and south toward my objective for the night, Riverton, Wyoming. This would place me about five and a half hours away from Denver, an easy drive to make before my flight the next afternoon. Most notably on this part of the drive, I stumbled upon the Red Gulch Dinosaur Tracksite, a government-run excavation and study area, the site of the Dinosaur's Ballroom, an area where one could plainly see dinosaur tracks preserved in cooled mud.

One had to leave this sparsely traveled highway and drive down a dirt road for five miles in order to get to this site. Once there, however, you could get out of your car and walk along a boardwalk to get to the footprints, and then go down into the Dinosaur's Ballroom and actually touch the tracks. This was a moving experience, knowing I was making contact with something that occurred more than 200 million years ago, and this was something for which I was particularly excited given my childhood love of dinosaurs. This mud, in other words, was a living witness to dinosaurs.

But truly more remarkable than this experience was what I discovered as I walked along this boardwalk. I was the only one at this site at this time of day (understandable, given it was the middle of a Wednesday). I realized as I walked along I heard nothing. Literally listening to nothing, as in no animal was making noises, there was no wind, certainly no man-made sounds. It was if I had gone deaf; there even was no white noise of any kind to provide a backdrop. In that moment, on that beautifully sunny day in the middle of a dinosaur track site I discovered purely by accident, my world was devoid of sound. It was an eerie feeling at first, but then I reveled in it. I closed my eyes and just stood still. Absolutely nothing. Maybe a cricket would chirp, and then the world was silent again. I felt like the only human left on the planet, as I had felt along much of that drive that day. I could look out and see towering, hazy mountains and plateaus, but then I'd close my eyes, and my senses would register nothing. Under what other circumstances would I again discover this sensation? It made me realize that even if we seek refuge in our "quiet time," we are never truly, purely, literally devoid of sound, even white noise. This was an awesome experience because it was so novel yet based on the simplest of things.

I have since come to believe the sound of "nothing" is actually the grand symphony of Mother Nature herself. In the silence, you can hear everything working in harmony, if you allow yourself to become peaceful and learn to listen. Humans have introduced the unexpected, grating sharps and flats that screech out of key against the score of Mother Nature's silent orchestra. The sound of humanity's noises — cars, factories, even man-made music — has no place in such a majestic musical arrangement. A motorcycle roaring down the highway is like having a clarinet out of key, instantly drawing attention to it instead of harmoniously contributing to the composition. In some places of this world, nature's melody has been replaced by these grating, out of key instruments. But in others, like this little spot in the middle of Wyoming, Maestro Mother Nature is still fully in control, and the orchestra plays on as if defective instruments had never been invented.

I drove the five miles back to the highway and continued on my southerly voyage. I got the sense that I was on a walkabout. Like I said, I felt like the only human on the planet. The imagery was out of a dream. Plateaus jutting out for seemingly miles and the cleanest air and skyline you could imagine. I drove through canyons with grades that reminded me of driving through Utah. I passed over the Continental Divide. I passed through Thermopolis, a town I had discovered previously on my Google Map search of what way to take to Riverton, and a town I wanted to pass through purely because I thought it was an awesome name. I passed through Shell, Wyoming, population 83 people. At one point I was driving straight to a plateau that seemed to reach so high as to be at right angles with the ground, like that scene in the movie *Inception* where the two characters walk onto a street that seemed to be folded up onto a right angle with the rest of the street. As those characters were in a dream, so I felt, as well. I was driving at such high elevations I felt closer to the heavens.

There might be some facts to support this feeling. Think about it: In Maine, particularly southern Maine, you drive normally at sea level or maybe a couple hundred feet above sea level. In Wyoming you could drive at 6,000 to 8,000 feet above sea level, so let's say maybe a mile and a half. So in Wyoming you are a mile and a half higher up in the air at any given time than what I would experience in Maine. My point is, maybe this was the reason I felt like I was in another world, or in a dream, while driving in Wyoming. The sky seemed closer — maybe this was actually true! I therefore felt more "squeezed" between the earth and the sky.

But maybe my welcome uneasiness was also due to the incredibly pristine nature of the land. The West truly is civilization's last chance to not mess up a good thing. We have desecrated the East Coast, polluted it, torn it up for our own industrial greed. The area from which my family came, northeastern New Jersey, is a prime example of this desecration. Here in Wyoming, where civilization seems so spread out and unassuming, the whole state feels like one big nature preserve. The normal here is a state of preservation, the exact opposite of the East Coast. Aha! Maybe I figured out why I felt so weird driving through this state; the situation was unlike anything I had experienced before, or at least was accustomed to perceiving. In Wyoming we hadn't looked at the land and immediately thought of how we could best exploit it. Whoever led the charge to preserve this land is a hero in my book.

"Vast pristineness." I think that's a good phrase to use. I know the Wyoming land, as I saw it, was probably exactly the same hundreds of millions of years ago. (Actually, one of the roadside stops on the way into the Bighorn National Forest remarked that this area used to be ocean, but you get my point.)

I landed in Riverton for the night. I went out to a local bar, the Bar Ten, looking to meet some locals and get some insight into what it is like living here. Nicely enough, it was easy to engage in conversation with two cousins who posted up at the bar next to me, but they were from Missouri originally, currently lived in Colorado, and one of them was moving to Houston to take a promotion in his current job as a US Department of Agriculture poultry and meat inspector. We made idle talk about Colorado and Wyoming and watched baseball highlights on ESPN.

The next morning, I left for the five-and-a-half-hour drive to Colorado. I passed much of the same terrain as I've already described. I got into Denver no problem and got on my flight.

I became more and more thankful for my job. It afforded me the opportunity to drive 1,000 miles around such a place as the American West. If someone had asked me if a dream job of mine would involve doing exactly what I did on this little road trip, I would have discarded the idea as too impractical. I never felt more reinforced in my belief that I made the absolute right decision when I took this job. And moreover, I realized how my hard work and dedication studying for the bar the second time came to pay off. Wow! Talk about a lesson in delayed gratification! To think that if I had failed a second time I was going to discard everything this job had to offer me and go find something that did not require bar passage. My alternate-universe self is bemoaning his inability to pass the bar. Even now, six months after taking the bar, I remember well the trials and tribulations, the emotional toll that marked the winter of 2018-2019 as I studied for that test again. The "five-month funk," as I described it to a friend.

I arrived home on August 21, immensely satisfied with my Wyoming trip. I realized it was my nirvana. Even on the plane home, I couldn't wait to go back.

**FOURTH WEEK OF AUGUST, 2019:** This week saw me travel to New Mexico from Monday until Wednesday. I left for New Mexico on Monday at 5:30 a.m., mere hours after arriving home from a Northport, Maine wedding Catherine and I attended. It was a rare opportunity to do something together! I was able to sleep well on the plane, and I arrived in New Mexico at 10:30 a.m. local time. Having almost the full day to kill, I hopped in my rental car and drove an hour and a half north to Santa Fe, on the outskirts of which was the Santa Fe National Forest. There I hiked the trail called Raven's Ridge. It was mostly a nature walk, but there was a serious incline that made me unusually light headed. I thought maybe I was not well-hydrated or that I was undernourished for the day, but then I realized that I was a little more than 11,000 feet in the air! I had never been so high. I had never gotten light-headed like that before.

I didn't think I would get to the true summit, so I declared victory after spending some time at one particularly scenic lookout, and then went back down the car. This national forest was just that, wooded, and it reminded me of home; therefore, it did not draw out the excitement I felt at seeing other "desert" locations, like in southeastern New Mexico and western Texas.

I finished this hike around 3 p.m. and drove half an hour away toward a site I didn't think to visit until I was looking at my AllTrails app: The Civil War's Glorietta Pass battlefield. This was the true gem of the trip. This March 1862 battle was technically a Confederate victory, but, as I learned, a strategic victory was handed to the Union army due to a daring flank attack by a Union contingent that destroyed the Confederates' supply train, forcing the Confederate army to retreat back into Texas and, therefore, saving the southwest for the Union. I had heard of this battlefield through my copious civil war study, but I had always written it off as a place I would never visit due to its distance from Maine and the East Coast battlefields, as well as the fact that I did not think the battlefield was well preserved or very big to begin with.

I was mostly wrong. The battle was small, but the field itself was well preserved. Informative markers were well-placed around a two and a half mile walking loop, which I mostly jogged. I learned a lot about the battlefield and was really glad I decided to hop over there before leaving the Santa Fe area. Talk about a deep cut! This battle pales when compared to Gettysburg or other famous battles, but it was called the "Gettysburg of the West" due to its importance to the overall strategic picture.

I had dinner in Santa Fe before heading back to Albuquerque, in a nice cantina-style restaurant called Maria's New Mexican Kitchen. I met a guy at the bar, Bill, who pointed to my Maine Marathon shirt and said, "You know it's so funny you walked in here, I was just telling these guys how Maine is my favorite vacation spot." It turns out he has visited Maine many times, and he particularly likes Camden — 40 minutes from my hometown — and the drive along the coast. What a small, small world.

My hearing on Tuesday morning went well and concerned George from Las Cruces, New Mexico. He was familiar with Alamogordo, the White Sands, the Organ Mountains, and the surrounding area. I told him again (the first time in our typical pre-hearing conference call), that I was thrilled to meet someone from that area because I have fallen in love with that part of the southwest desert. I told him of my first visit in June, my road trip with Bill in July, and my desire to go again as soon as possible. I even told him about my association between the Organ Mountains and *Moonlight Motel* and my insistence on visiting the Thunder Road overlook of Alamogordo. He appreciated the connection as he said he was a Springsteen fan himself. He is a kind man who had been fighting his claim for PTSD for several years. He witnessed a ship sink that was carrying many of his friends and comrades. He was the last man not allowed on this ship, as the crew was coming from liberty leave to be shuttled to their main ship. He not only witnessed the accidental crash that caused the deaths of 49 of the 110 soldiers onboard, but he afterward participated in the recovery efforts. Ever since he has been battling survivor's guilt, depression, and other signs of PTSD. He expressed the frustration and confusion he had at the VA for not officially recognizing his stressor. He took the VA's restrictive criteria to succeed on PTSD cases as a personal affront, akin to the VA thinking he was lying about the ship accident.

The hearing went well, but it was obvious George had a tough time telling the judge about his experiences. However, like Philip in Nebraska and all of these clients, his courage in seeking help was inspiring.

After the hearing, I walked out of the hearing room with George. We had to sign some paperwork for the firm, so he sat down in the waiting room and tried to balance the papers on his knee. As he was writing his gaze slowly shifted away from the papers, his glistening eyes settling on the far wall. His pen slowly came to a rest. He sighed and said to me, "Sometimes . . . I even wonder if I am telling the truth. Did it really happen?"

I explained that his case had been unsuccessful so far not because the VA did not believe him, but that the VA had not yet "checked all the boxes" in order to award him compensation benefits. For the reader's benefit, there is a simple reason why a PTSD claim is harder to win than almost any other disability claim: the claim requires a "verified" stressor. This means that the veteran has to prove to the VA, through documentation or in some cases testimony, that they did indeed witness or experience an event and that the event happened in the first place. So in George's case, he had not yet proven to the VA that his ship did indeed sink, that he had friends on it, and that he personally witnessed the event. Almost every other disability claim — including non-PTSD mental health issues like depression or anxiety — *do not require* a "verified stressor." So some free legal advice: If you know a veteran who is applying for VA compensation benefits and suffers from some mental health issue, make sure they claim benefits for "any acquired psychiatric disorder," not just PTSD.

In early 2020 I learned the result of George's case. The judge agreed with my argument that George's PTSD claim should be read as a claim for "any acquired psychiatric disorder," which is permissible because the VA does not have any "strict pleading" claim requirements, and granted his claim for service connection! I clearly remember running through an airport, taking a moment to call George with the result. He was so relieved on the principle of the matter: that the VA conceded service connection in some way. He was so grateful for my help and the work the firm did on his case. The VA eventually awarded him only a 30 percent rating, which both George and myself thought was too low. So the appeal goes on . . .

After the hearing I had most of the afternoon left, so I went to hike the Eye of the Sandrias trail on the outskirts of Albuquerque. This was a significantly lower elevation than the Santa Fe National Forest, only 6,000 to 7,000 feet high, but it afforded a spectacular view of the city. Remarkably, the city was so laid out that it was tough to tell that it was indeed a major city. No tall buildings cluttered the landscape, and there were sufficient trees and other vegetation around, such that, at least at that elevation, the individual houses and buildings were tough to see. This contrasted with the East Coast cities I was used to, which are generally built up and less spread out.

Thus ended the first three months of this travel job. By my rough estimation, I had hearings in 16 different states through these first three months, with probably somewhere around 16 to 20 hearings total. My favorite place so far, if you couldn't tell, is Wyoming, narrowly beating out the southeastern part of New Mexico and western Texas. My least favorites were Los Angeles, Montgomery, and Florida.

On my way home, sitting in the Baltimore Airport, I wrote a poem about the effect hiking has on me. I hope this will help the reader understand why I seek out mountains wherever I go. I called it "Lessons from a Mountain Top."

*If I ruled the world,*
*would I do it from here?*
*Where the blue sky and slight wind*
*Make it all seem so clear?*

*If I ruled the world,*
*Would I ever come down?*
*Or would I wave forever*
*At the little ants running around?*

*Even if I didn't rule the world,*
*If I wanted to get away,*
*I'd go hike the nearest horizon*
*All leave all my fears at bay.*

*And when I get to the top, settle down,*
*Cast my gaze to the sky so clear,*
*The world would seem so very vast*
*From my little perch up here.*

*So here I sit*
*Not a care in my head*
*And civilization far away.*

*You'd better bet,*
*I'll never come down.*
*I'd stay up here all day.*

FALL

# SEPTEMBER 2019

**FIRST WEEK OF SEPTEMBER, 2019:** This week brought me to Roanoke, Virginia, then to Pittsburgh, Pennsylvania, via a drive through the Shenandoah Valley. I was excited for this trip, coming off a five-day respite at home. Even after such a relatively short time, I was ready to get back on the road. I flew into Roanoke without difficulty, jumped in my rental car, and set my GPS to Dragon's Tooth Trail, a "hard" hiking trail I found on AllTrails. This hike was spectacular. It was a challenging nature hike, at the end of which was a rock protrusion that makes the Dragon Tooth name understandable. I enjoyed sitting at the top of this rock formation, the very top of which was probably not meant to be climbed. It was serene and reminded me of the poem I recite at the end of my last entry. It was a beautiful day to hike, and the view from the top afforded me nice views of surrounding greenery, rolling mountains, and rustic farmland.

This day was most memorable because of the place I went for dinner after my hike. It was a bar called "Mac and Bobs" in Salem, Virginia. It attracted my attention because of its good reviews on Google. I posted up at the bar (as opposed to sitting at a table, which I never do when eating alone) one seat over from a solitary guy drinking a glass of wine. We got to chatting. He was a 22-year old Egyptian named Mohemmed. He was a double major international student at a local university. He had left Egypt for the American dream. He would have been persecuted in Egypt for having different political views and for being bisexual. He said he had ADHD and tried to excuse himself for being so talkative to a stranger. No problem in my book!

I think it helped that he was on his second or third glass of wine, which somehow paired well with the chicken wings he was having for dinner.

He started to tear up when talking about people who helped him deal with his attention deficiency. Obviously, these people have had such a big impact on him. He spoke not with effusive praise, filled with gesticulations or high tones. Instead, he was solemn and tried to stifle tears (which his emotional intensity and wine consumption precluded from effectively doing). I think he misunderstood the *kind* of disabilities I work with (physical, emotional, and mental over intellectual or cognitive), but his praise for my job was deeply impactful and moved me.

He couldn't thank me enough for pursuing this kind of career. He reassured me that my clients appreciate it so much as well. He also teared up at the freedom we have in America. The freedom to think, say, and do what we want.

I am thrilled that he was able to come to America and loves living here. His story is the kind that makes one forget about the seemingly important — *i.e.* the antics and embarrassments of President Trump, which I could never escape hearing about — and instead makes those issues seem trivial. Hearing stories like his draws attention to what truly makes American great, the freedom to try and live, think, and thrive in any way someone sees fit. This freedom and liberty to live your life is the promise of America. He left the bar before I did and remarked again how glad he was to meet me. The feeling was most definitely mutual.

He volunteered that he was extremely proud of himself for coming as far as he had given his upbringing and place of origin. He wholeheartedly accepted my comment that I was proud of him too. He made an enigma of an encounter. Here he was at a massive bar, sitting alone, sipping a glass of wine while ravishing an order of wings. I hope I will continue to remember the conversations we had.

After the three hearings I had the next morning, I started for Pittsburgh, Pennsylvania. The drive was not as scenic as I had hoped. The lower Shenandoah Valley was mostly flat and afforded little view beyond the trees that lined the highway. It was a straight shot up the highway to a point about 40 miles to the east of Pittsburgh, at which point I jumped on the Pennsylvania turnpike, arriving in Pittsburgh around 8 p.m. I was feeling antsy from sitting in the car and the VA hearing waiting room, so I jumped on the treadmill despite the late hour. My two hearings the next day went well, and I was able to get home around dinner time, unlike the many times I flew into Portland at 11:30 p.m. at night.

So far, I've told the reader what I do on my various excursions, but I would forgive you for asking the question: What did you do in airports and airplanes? It's a fair question. In airports and on airplanes is where I spent the majority of any day I traveled.

The answer is fairly simple: Thank god for smartphones. On my phone I could watch streaming services, read, hone my German language skills through Duolingo, talk with friends and family, and, importantly, set an alarm, so I could sleep and not miss my flight. I said before that I can sleep anywhere. The reader must take this literally: on the floor of airports (more on that later), in a squished airplane seat, sitting up, you name it. My travels were made far less tedious than they could have been if I could not automatically sleep on airplanes. At no other time was my ease of travel on display than the second week of September 2019.

**SECOND WEEK OF SEPTEMBER 2019:** This week saw me leave Portland, Maine, for a hearing in White City, Oregon. Then I drove up to Portland, Oregon, for a one-day NOVA (National Organization of Veterans' Advocates) conference, and then flew to Burlington, Vermont for a one-day visit with College Bill.

The September 11, 2019 hearing in White City went well and ahead of schedule. I was able to get on the road to Portland around 9:30 a.m. This was best as I elected to take a slower, more scenic route than straight up I-5, which I had done twice before. This new route took six hours, but it took me through Bend, Oregon, and the Mount Hood National Forest. All throughout my drive I was impressed with how tree-covered the route was, and I got some good views of the 11,000-foot-tall Mount Hood. I stopped at the Timberline Lodge, the site of many movie shoots, including exterior shoots in *The Shining*. The weather was beautiful, and of course it was reminiscent of Maine. I arrived in Portland around 5 p.m. and met Uncle Evan and his girlfriend, Ashley, at a great Thai place for dinner. We spent dinner mostly talking about my upcoming wedding, then still scheduled for June 2020. Afterwards, we went to a great bookstore called City of Books, where I bought a 1968 copy of *The Making of Star Trek*, written to describe the production history of the original series. It was a great find and only cost three dollars.

The next day, NOVA had their basic session, which covered the fundamentals of service connection, increased ratings, etc. Besides a nice refresher course on the various legal principles I used in my hearings, the conference was notable because it gave me an opportunity to further bond with fellow attorneys at Jackson and MacNichol, something I don't often get to do being on the road. While sitting in one of the presentations, one of my co-workers learned she passed the bar! We went to a fancy Italian place for dinner in celebration.

After the September 12 one-day NOVA session, I left early in the morning on September 13 to fly to Burlington, Vermont, for a prearranged weekend visit with College Bill. I spent only a day with him, but it was a pretty full day.

Bill picked me up at the Burlington airport at 11 p.m. We sat out on his porch until probably 1:30 a.m. We primarily talked about my wedding. I woke up at 10:30 a.m. the next morning. I cannot remember the last time I slept in that late, almost surely also due to such rapid travel between coasts. We decided to go out and hike Mount Mansfield, despite the rain, wind, and slippery conditions of the trail. Basically, every factor worked against us, but we, unsafely, went out anyway. Roots were wet, rocks were slippery, I had no tread on my worn-down shoes, and moss was everywhere. Despite this — or maybe because of this — we had a grand time. We had a few slips and falls, and the lack of a view was disappointing, but we were still doing something we both liked, and liked doing together.

We arrived back in Burlington around dinner time and vociferously consumed a pizza at Manhattan's. We sat at the window bar and people watched as we ate — a past time I turned to often while on the road. We then went back to his apartment and had a quiet night. Instead of going out to the indie rock festival Bill had proposed, we decided to just stay in and play *Grand Theft Auto*, a strong nostalgic throwback to our shared college days. A tumultuous music festival versus a quiet night in — it's a wonder we get along as well as we do.

I later told Bill I would enjoy looking back on this particular weekend as an example of just how active my life was while I did this travel job. On Tuesday, September 10, I flew from Maine to Oregon. On Wednesday I drove six hours to get from Medford to Portland, Oregon. On Thursday I had a conference in Portland. On Friday I flew from Portland to Burlington, spent only a day in Burlington, and then endured another West Coast flight to get to California (as described below). I could phrase my travels that week in a couple different ways: I had two West Coast flights over the course of only six days. I so looked forward to seeing Bill that I traveled however many hours and endured the time difference just to see him for a day. I'm proud of myself for willingly doing this kind of travel. It was intense and not for everyone, but I truly enjoyed it. I always had to be in motion. No wonder I got antsy whenever I was back in Maine for as little as a week or so. And then before that travel week was up, I flew again to Oklahoma from California. At least this was an incremental time difference! But I am getting ahead of myself.

**THIRD WEEK OF SEPTEMBER, 2019:** I awoke at 3:55 a.m. to catch an Uber ride to the Burlington airport. At 5 a.m. I was on a plane heading back to the West Coast, the second time in five days. I was going to Sacramento, California, where I had a hearing in nearby Rancho Cordova. This Monday, September 16 hearing required diligence and direct questioning, unlike other hearings I had. The client tended to ramble, and I had to work hard to make sure his testimony stayed focused. I had to get down to the heart of the matter – that his foot was injured in an engine room accident – and keep to a minimum the other kinds of irrelevant information he wanted to add, like how the machinery in the engine room worked and why he was stationed in the engine room in the first place. To achieve this goal, I had to ask cross-examination kinds of questions – those which required only a "yes" or a "no." This kind of questioning was frowned upon by judges because the proceeding's nature was supposed to be unlike that of your stereotypical "courtroom" experience; instead, it was much more relaxed and conversational. At the end of hearing the client and his wife were relieved to be done and profusely thanked me and the firm for representing them. I was thankful for the opportunity to shake up my typical hearing experience so far. Maybe there was a future for me in litigation!

On the advice of my client, I drove two hours north to visit Paradise, California. My client lived in Paradise until being displaced by the wildfire that engulfed that area in November 2018. He stated this fire was so intense that it created its own "fire tornado" and burned the surrounding area at the rate of 80 acres a minute. As I was searching for something to do, I committed to the two-hour drive, figuring I could find a place to hike up there. My plan to hike in the Eldorado National Forest, west of Rancho Cordova, was sidetracked by bad weather. The destruction of Paradise was total and devastating, and a visitor could certainly tell the area was hit hard and struggling to get back on its feet. I came across one standing tree that was charred on one side yet pristine on the other. I drove past destroyed gas stations devoid of pumps or business, collapsed buildings and piles of rubble. Despite this, there were signs of resurgence. Inspirational signs were placed around the destroyed town. Construction workers were busy repairing roadways and half-standing buildings.

I jumped on the AllTrails app to find a good hiking spot. I settled on a route called Lil Falls Trail, in northern Paradise. This was labeled as a great trail jogging route. I was very impressed with it. The trail was wide open, but it was apparent that you were running/walking through a forest that was rebuilding itself. It was so peaceful, quiet, and serene. The trail was 4.4 miles round trip, and I mostly trail ran it. The trail had a little waterfall. The poetic possibilities were seemingly endless. "Desolation in Paradise," "Running through Paradise," "Paradise Reborn," etc.

The next morning, I flew to Tulsa, Oklahoma, as I had a hearing in Musk-
ogee on September 18. Oklahoma appears to be a boring place — very
flat, fast food-filled, and devoid of entertainment except such things as
amusement parks, water parks, etc. I bet it's interesting for many people,
but it's not a place I would go on vacation. This was the first hearing where
I walked away not being at least reasonably confident of the eventual out-
come. This was mostly due to the client impeaching himself by contradict-
ing himself on some aspects of his Thailand service, a critical component
of his Agent Orange claims. His daughter tearfully described to the judge
how she thought her father's contradictions were due to his decreased mental state, PTSD symptoms, and age. But I think I salvaged what I could
and certainly at least some of the nine claims on appeal were meritorious.
In early 2020, the judge released an entirely favorable decision. The judge
utilized the unique "benefit of the doubt" doctrine, a rule in VA law that
allows the judge to award benefits when the evidence for and against the
veteran "is in equipoise." In other words, "tie goes to the runner."

I flew home eight days after leaving Maine. I felt weary but proud of the
travels and work I had done over the past week. I looked forward to seeing
Catherine, friends, and family. My social calendar was full until the next
week. This eight-day stint reinforced for me that personality-wise, I always
have to be moving on to the next thing. I have to keep moving. I was gone
for eight days but I only had three hearings and a day of the NOVA conference. The rest was laborious travel, *i.e.* the long drive in Oregon or the
cross-country flights, but I still wouldn't have traded it for anything

At this point, I reflected how this job impacted my health. It is *very* hard
to eat well and exercise regularly when always on airplanes. I had gained a
few pounds over the three and a half months, not bad for eating out literally every meal. I also credited the exercise regime I maintained while on
the road. I sat on planes many days, but at every opportunity I tried to get
outside. When outdoor activity was not practical, I enjoyed going on the
hotel treadmills. My emotional health remained good as well. Yes, I missed
Catherine, friends, and family terribly while I was gone, but my depressed
feelings stayed away as long as I had fun activities to keep me busy. My
spirits were usually buoyed by the positive reactions I got from veterans.

They usually couldn't stop professing their appreciation at what the firm does for them. I reciprocated that feeling more than I could convey.

**FOURTH WEEK OF SEPTEMBER, 2019:** This week brought me to Seattle, Washington, a three-day visit in Atlanta, and then a return home. The Seattle trip was notable because I was able to visit my college friends, Sebastian and Kelsey. We met up at a pizza place in nearby Issaquah, about equidistant for them coming from Carnation and me coming from my hotel in Renton. I had not seen them for more than two and a half years, and we spent about three hours together. It was a fun visit over some of the best chicken and pesto pizza I have ever had. They invited me to hang out again on one of the two other trips I was making to Seattle in October.

My hearing concerned a memorable client. His name was Matthew. He was a 68-year-old Navy veteran who lives in Tacoma, Washington. On the conference call I had with Matthew a week before the hearing, and in the hearing itself, he broke down crying, describing the various in-service events that we thought caused his mental health issues. He witnessed a couple airplane incidents in which two of his comrades were killed, and their deaths were shown indifference by their superiors. For the 50 years after these incidents he has suffered greatly as he has never trusted anyone enough to tell them the story of his stressors. His wife died, and he has no kids, so he lives alone, further compounding his distress. I had never heard a client so thoroughly and easily break down describing their service. This was more than shedding a tear or choking up; his shoulders heaved and his face grew red as he lost his composure. At the end of our conference call I informed him that the VA provides free psychiatric counseling for veterans in exactly his situation. He had no idea and was lifted by this new prospect of help. When I saw him in Seattle a week later, the first thing he did was show me a piece of paper he pulled from his wallet. It had a date, time, and place on it. He informed me he had an appointment with a VA counselor and was looking forward to talking with someone about his issues. Perhaps more than a victory on his compensation benefits — the judge's decision about which would come, if we were lucky, in six months — I was thrilled that I was able to help Matthew this way. He was getting *immediate* relief. He could use the benefits, but he *needed* the counseling. I'm thrilled he was so willing to seek out care. I think he felt a renewed sense of life purpose in seeking treatment, like there was some way he could tackle his PTSD symptoms besides by himself.

I was very proud of Matthew regarding how he handled himself in the hearing. We were prepared for what I thought was the eventuality of him breaking down so thoroughly as to not be able to get through his testimony. But through tears and some pauses, Matthew thoroughly described the stressors in as sufficient detail as I wanted, without prompting by myself. He described his struggles since the service and his willingness to seek help now. Before we went off the record, I made sure to note how proud I was of his courage and how he rose to the occasion. As we walked out together and parted ways on the sidewalk, he expressed his gratitude toward me and the firm. I expressed how it was an honor to meet him and how glad I was I was able to make the trip out to represent him. I looked forward to following this case and making sure I do everything I can to earn him the benefits he deserves. I am humbled to have helped him out so much, both during and before the hearing.

After the hearing, I bucked the adverse weather forecasts and decided to go hiking. I picked Rattlesnake Mountain, about 30 miles east from Renton. I did two different hikes. The first one started at around 12 p.m. and was marred by fog and mist. This unique hiking weather, however, made for some interesting pictures, and the end of it brought me very nearly face-to-face with a deer. I was walking down the path, randomly looked to my left, and there was this large deer, with antlers, not more than 15 feet from me, standing frozen staring at me. I froze for only a moment, when two thoughts led me to dart behind a tree: (1) that deer has antlers; and (2) I am defenseless. I know deer are not normally aggressive, but the fact remained that if that deer wanted to, he could have done serious injury to me, and with such a relatively close distance between us, he could react much faster than I could. I retreated down the path.

As I finished this hike, the clouds miraculously parted, presenting clear skies and nearly perfect weather all around. Exhausted, yet not willing to give up what turned out to be a great day, I turned to Google Maps to find another nearby hike I could do. I found something called Stan's Overlook on the other side of Rattlesnake Mountain, which appeared more rightly to be a large ridge. I trail ran most of this trail, but it did not present a great view despite the name, leaving me slightly disappointed. It was a great exercise day, though, as each hike was about four miles round trip. The first hike was about 1,100 feet in elevation gain. I got coffee at the Issaquah Coffee Company on the way back to my hotel. Early the next morning, September 28, I flew to Atlanta, Georgia.

Even though I have had *many* layovers in Atlanta (Concourse B quickly became my home away from home), this was my first time leaving the airport. Georgia is probably my favorite southeastern state; this trip only reinforced that view. I arrived in Atlanta around 9 p.m. at night, and the next morning, September 29, I went out to the Kennesaw Mountain National Battlefield. This battlefield is about 30 minutes north of Atlanta and marks a June 1964 Civil War battlefield fought during Sherman's March to Atlanta. I had no idea this battlefield was so well preserved. It was the largest battle of the Atlanta campaign, and it was one of the few confederate victories in the western theater of war. This battlefield was perfect for me: so many hiking trails, under tree cover, and large enough that I could take a whole day to explore if I had the time. I hiked a five-mile trail from Kennesaw Mountain to Little Kennesaw Mountain and Pigeon Hill, and down to Cheatham Hill, where most of the battle was fought. This last marker featured what is called The Dead Angle, the site of a particularly gruesome part of the battle. This hike was beautiful, affording some view, though more importantly it was under tree cover, which I appreciated in the 95-degree heat. This hike thoroughly exhausted me; I was coming off a lot of jet lag and was not used to the humidity. I rested for a bit before getting an Uber to get back to my rental car.

That night, I met up with a high school friend, Eric, whom I hadn't seen since 2012. It was truly a blast from the past to see him again. Originally from Albuquerque, he attended my high school for a semester in 2010. We had dinner together and caught up for about two hours. We parted hoping I would soon get to Atlanta again.

# OCTOBER 2019

———◆◆———

**FIRST WEEK OF OCTOBER, 2019:** This week was remarkably uneventful. I had a hearing in Roanoke, VA, on October 3, but my client did not show! The office's and my attempts to get in touch with him were unsuccessful. I therefore made the trip for nothing. It was such a quick visit to begin with that I did not make time to go for a hike or enjoy the beautiful southwestern Virginia mountains, on what turned out to be a gorgeous couple of days. Instead, I spent most of my time in the small Roanoke airport. This was the first time a client did not show up for his hearing with me. I spoke with the client when I got home, and he thought the hearing was on another day of the week. Such is the risk we run by sending attorneys out to meet clients at their home regional offices.

**SECOND WEEK OF OCTOBER, 2019:** This week saw me spend three days in Seattle, Washington. It was a long trip for one hearing, but the hearing went well. When I flew in, I immediately checked into the hotel, and then took advantage of the beautiful day by driving 20 minutes north of my hotel and going for a trail run/walk in a nearby preservation area.

The day of the hearing was similarly beautiful, so after my hearing I hiked the Poo Poo Trail, in nearby Issaquah, which had been recommended to me by my college friend Sebastian. This hike was about 7.5 miles round trip, had an elevation of around only 1,700 feet, but afforded a magnificent view of the highway, Issaquah itself, nearby mountains, and Seattle in the background. I sat at the top of this mountain, in a large clearing, and enjoyed the sun, watching paragliders take off and fly around the area. These paragliders were fun to watch. I was mesmerized, watching them seemingly float in one place or in little circles, enjoying the beautiful view. One group was there for a girl's birthday. The contraption these paragliders used was seemingly simple, a pouch in which to sit and belts used at arm's length to control the direction of the glider. I sat for a while envying the carefree-ness with which these paragliders operated their craft. They were leaves on the wind. One guy, however, seemed to have a hard time on takeoff. He dropped down from the cliff, disappearing from sight momentarily, and then emerged victorious above the cliff, fully in control of what he was doing.

The flight home was hell. This was the first time in the four months I had been traveling that I had to stay overnight in an airport because of a delay. My American Airlines connector flight out of Charlotte was delayed 11 times over the night between Friday and Saturday, ostensibly for mechanical issues. This caused me much angst because I was supposed to leave Westbrook at 8:40 a.m. with Catherine and law school friends to drive four hours north to Presque Isle for a law school classmate's wedding. I spent the night shivering on the floor of the Charlotte B terminal, waiting for my flight.

As my flight was consistently delayed without any assurance that the delays were permanent, I did not leave the airport to get a hotel room. Spending the night in an airport is downright weird. I had no "camp out" clothes, so I used my backpack as a pillow and my suit jacket as a blanket. I was only able to sleep a total of two hours. I would wake up every half hour or so because an arm was going numb, my back was sore from lying on the ground, or I was cold. I was shocked at how mean and rude passengers were to customer service representatives. I know emotions run high during such egregious flight delays — I myself was apoplectic that I was probably going to miss the wedding of two good law school friends. But I knew that the flight delays were not the customer service representatives' fault. When I approached one looking to see my alternative flight options, the first thing I said to her was, "Please don't worry. I'm not going to yell at you. I know this delay isn't your fault." The depth of her sign of relief was an unfortunate indicator of how poorly she had been treated that night. Ultimately, the only other option for me was to fly into Bangor, Maine, around 10:30 a.m. in the morning, and hope that Catherine could time her arrival to pick me up in Bangor and get to Presque Isle in time for the wedding. I elected to not pursue this option, however, because it would have meant a change of flight fee of more than $500. I knew I was playing with the firm's money, so I didn't want to choose this option without at least first running it by my boss, which I couldn't do given the late time. I therefore stayed with my currently booked flight, hoping it would take off in time to land in Portland as early as possible.

At 5 a.m. the flight boarded for Portland. At last, we were on our way! Then the pilot came over the intercom. This plane also had a mechanical issue necessitating a delay! People started cursing, groaning, and cursing some more. I was sure I was going to miss the wedding. Everyone was downtrodden and infuriated. We all had to deplane and wait in the airport again. American Airlines found another plane, and we eventually lifted off at 7 a.m. I remember clearly my elation when we finally took off. I couldn't believe it!

As we were waiting for the plane to take off, the woman sitting next to me turned to me, a quizzical look on her face, and said, "I'm sorry to bother you, but you look so familiar." I thought for the moment, then it hit me.

"Yes!" I said. "You are a consultant for a law firm in Maine . . . a vocational consultant, or something like that, right?"

"Yeah!" she exclaimed. "And you're the lawyer!"

I couldn't believe the coincidence. I sat next to this very same woman on a different flight home a couple months before. We got to talking, but like many airplane conversations, we learned about each other but never really got each other's names. Now, here she was again. What are the chances? The very same person on different flights, at different times, from different airports but the same destination — home.

As it turns out the Bangor flight was delayed much longer than the Portland-bound flight, reinforcing my decision to stick with my original plan. I arrived in Portland at 9:20 a.m., where Catherine and my law school friends were waiting for me. I literally ran through the airport, jumped in the car, and we ended up arriving in Presque Isle *five minutes* before the wedding started. Everything eventually worked out, but this flight permanently turned me off to American Airlines and temporarily lessened my excitement for my travel. I realized this could happen more often, but I considered myself lucky that with all the travel I did, this was the first time I was held up overnight by a delayed flight. I haven't flown American Airlines since.

**THIRD WEEK OF OCTOBER, 2019:** This week saw me revitalize my excitement for the travel part of my job due to a four-day visit to southwest Texas — the desert again! My travel morale had reached an all-time low after my disastrous experience the previous weekend. I had a hearing in San Antonio on Friday, so I flew down Thursday night to El Paso, rented a car, drove six hours to San Antonio, and continued from San Antonio to Big Bend National Park, where I spent the day on Saturday. I flew home Sunday. I could not pass up the opportunity for another West Texas road trip.

I thought the trip was off to a slow start when I drove from El Paso to San Antonio. It was nice being back in the desert, but I didn't get any of the really scenic views of the desert like I was hoping for. Maybe I was becoming jaded to the desert? I surely hoped not. I didn't feel like socializing, but I forced myself to stop for dinner at a bar, instead of continuing on my journey and eating dinner in the car. I'm glad I stopped, for I settled on a place called the Hitching Post Steakhouse, where I made conversation with a pipeline worker named Eric. Eric lived in Washington state but worked down here in Texas for months at a time doing pipeline work. He said he had a wife, and it was awful not seeing her more often. I could definitely relate, but certainly not on the kind of scale Eric had to live with. His story made me feel lucky I got to see Catherine every week, even if only for an evening or early in the morning crossing paths between work. The bar was interesting because it wasn't really a bar, it was a "club," incorporated as such because the county does not allow consumption of liquor on premises. Therefore, people technically have to join this club in order to buy alcohol. Furthermore, this club allowed smoking in the bar. I didn't think I had been in a restaurant that allowed smoking since I was a kid, before the Maine law banning smoking in restaurants took effect.

The hearing went well, and I continued south to Del Rio, my first way-point on the way to Big Bend National Park. I felt on this drive that I was really getting into the southern part of the state; small towns dotted the highway, none more than a few buildings. I felt this way again driving from Alpine to El Paso. I had dinner in Del Rio — which was only a few miles from the Mexican border — and then continued on to Alpine, one of the closest towns to Big Bend. This drive was fascinating. I threw on *Western Stars* and enjoyed the scenery matching the music. The sweeping orchestra in songs like "Chasing Wild Horses" matched the sweeping nature of the landscape around me. The road to Alpine was so desolate; it was the kind of desert I really enjoyed seeing, and it sparked the excitement in me that was neutered in this trip's beginning. This desert reminded me of how excited I was driving through Utah on my cross-country trip. I felt so alone in the vastness. The desert certainly has a way of humbling someone. It seems hard to believe that a mile in the desert is the same as a mile in the wilderness. In Maine you can go a mile and have to negotiate several turns, deal with trees that block the line of sight, and deal with other encumbrances that make you think a mile is actually longer than it is. In the desert, however, you can see straight in front of you for many miles. You can have the same plateau accompanying you for an hour — it's either so big or so far away that it remains in your vision, a constant companion while traveling alone. I don't think you could get anything like that surrounded by trees. I couldn't help but itch to explore every part of the desert that unfolded before me, to climb every mountain. As the night progressed, I chased the setting red and yellow sun — I almost didn't mind that I would never catch it. Just for the hell of it I went 110 miles an hour on one stretch of road, just because I could and felt like I wasn't endangering anyone or anything. Later on though, I got caught for going 84 in a 75. A Brewster County police officer let me off with a warning.

I will always remember the Saturday I spent in Big Bend National Park. This national park straddles the Texas-Mexico border and is billed as one of the most isolated national parks in the country. It took two hours to get to the park from Alpine — my kind of place! Only one little north-south state route connected the park with the Texas state route that ran east to west about two hours north of the park entrance. I drove in during sunrise as I wanted to maximize the time spent in the park. I knew I would only get one day, and who knows when I would be back (but that's what I said about the Organ Mountains!). Seeing the sun rise above the mountains was truly majestic — the bright orange and red colors blanketed across the vast landscape, making for an awe-inspiring scene. I pulled over at one point so I could take in the view. I set out for the most strenuous hike in the park, Emery Peak, a 7,500-foot mountain, along a 10.5-mile hiking route, with 2,500 feet of elevation gain. On the way up I encountered a couple who was slowly and quietly retreating down the trail, as they had crossed paths with a couple bears who were making their way down the mountain. However, I had come too far and was too intent to give up my goal of reaching the top. I was going to proceed along myself, but thankfully, another hiker, Joe from Houston, came up behind me and offered to accompany me for the next mile or so, until we thought we were clear of where the bears were spotted. We each loaded up a free hand with rocks, in case we had to defend ourselves, and cautiously proceeded up the mountain. We didn't even get a peek at a bear, but it's probably a good idea we were as cautious as we were.

The top of this peak reminded me of the top of Guadelupe Peak. They are of similar heights and overlook the same terrain. I sat up there for maybe half an hour before I got antsy and needed to move on. I met a group of similarly aged young men from New York and New Jersey. I sat on a perch on the highest part of the peak. The rock at this particular location was seemingly molded into the shape of a chair — a captain's chair from which I felt fully in control of my surroundings and able to see everything. I made sure to take time to just soak in the view. I felt slightly queasy seeing birds flying below me. These birds zipped by like jet planes, making a sharp, doppler effect–type sound every time they swooshed by. Watching them dart around the rocks and around each other was disorienting, and I made sure to keep a firm footing on the rock.

I finished the hike around 12 p.m. After I descended the mountain, I drove along a 30-mile scenic driving route that ended at a canyon, through which the Rio Grande flowed. I was more excited to see this river than I had thought; in fact at the beginning of this trip I did not make any plans to see the river. I had only decided to go after I looked at the national park map and saw that I could kill two birds with one stone by driving down this scenic road to the Rio Grande. I was fascinated that I was at the extreme southern border of the United States and that I was dipping my hand into a river I had read so much about given my love of history.

Furthermore, I elected to try a quick 1.8-mile trail that would take me into the canyon itself. I decided to take the time to do this, even though it was around 3 p.m. and I wanted to get back into Alpine before dark. It turns out that on this trail you actually have to ford the Rio Grande. So I took off my shoes and socks and carefully waded across the extraordinarily muddy and murky water. I put my cell phone, headphones, and socks in my shoes, and carried my shoes across, a smile across my face the whole time. The mud enveloped my legs as I walked, with my feet sinking deep into the cool, encasing mud. I felt some hard objects if I sank my feet deep enough, maybe sticks? Or bones? Whatever they were, I was not freaked out, maybe because I knew that it was this area where officials expected people to cross, therefore making the crossing location reasonably safe. I also observed other tourists ford the river, so I figured it was more than reasonably safe for me to go as well.

After you emerge on the other side you can walk a short distance into the mouth of the canyon, which rose so high above, I felt like I was tilting my head up to look at a skyscraper. I was perplexed by this canyon. What an awesome force of nature that this water could slowly degrade the rock enough to form such a tall monument to nature. This canyon can be described as a "natural library bookshelf." As you worked your way from the bottom, and if you dug deep enough, you would find fossilized remains of various kinds of river-dwelling fish, mammals, or other types of life.

Nearer the top of the canyon the fossils would be thousands of years old. One would just have to skim the "book shelf" and could be looking at a fossilized witness to thousands of years of natural development. That's why in some areas of the park, and at the below mentioned dinosaur exhibit, markers would quickly point out that a particular fossil or sand formation "bore witness" to dinosaurs. This "witness" observation was also noted at the dinosaur "ballroom" site I stumbled upon in Wyoming. I thought I would just drive up to a river, but not the case! There were small boating and paddle-boating parties floating the river — young men whooping and hollering. What fun they must have had!

On the way out of the park I stopped at a dinosaur-fossil exhibit. Apparently, Big Bend is one of the most popular areas for paleontology, as this region was home to many kinds of dinosaurs across various time periods. I hoped to see active dig sites, but the "exhibit" was more of a mini-museum dedicated to explaining what kind of dinosaurs lived in the Big Bend area and when and how Big Bend turned into the arid desert it is now. (Like areas I visited in Wyoming, it was a large ocean hundreds of millions of years ago.) The next day, I drove the remaining three hours to El Paso, fully satisfied with the fullness of this trip and thrilled with the effort I put in. As expected, the drive saw the same open desert terrain I have come to love and hope I do not become jaded towards anytime soon.

I have tried to explain the effect the desert has on me, often with little success. I have often said I do not possess the necessary vocabulary to adequately explain my thoughts on the issue. At this point in my journal I took some time to brainstorm by stream of consciousness:

> I can understand why centuries of young men have fallen in love with the desert. Why the desert became a land of opportunity for economically ravaged families looking for a change; why Americans thought it was their Manifest Destiny to expand across the plains, deserts, and ultimately link the two North American coasts under one flag. The desert is vast; as I described above, one mile in the desert seems much more significant than one mile anywhere else. Everything's bigger in the desert — the mountains, the road

trips, the opportunities for one to get away from it all. Not that getting away from it all is ever a goal of mine, but I have to admit that I enjoy long stretches through the desert when my cell phone signal disappears. The desert is freedom. When I am in the desert, my horizons are only limited by the actual horizon. Yet at the same time, I feel like life stands still, maybe because there is so little physical movement when looking out over a desert plain. I love this feeling. I love how the desert is not "busy" like anything else touched by humans. No moving cars, people, anything! Just life standing still. This is a majestic and *unusual* feeling — maybe the unusualness forms part of my draw to the desert. These mountains I long to climb were there long before I lived and will be there long after I die.

The desert stands still regardless of ownership, of political strife, and is non-partisan in the difficulties they present a young voyager. There is certainly poetry to the desert's architecture, free from the ugliness of humanity's destructive mark on Earth's natural resources. City versus desert is "humanity's design" versus "God's design." There is a reason they call the desert "God's Country"; it is so untouched by humans, and I hope it stays that way. Can it be possibly by *only* random happenstance that the magnificence of the desert formed the way it formed? Is it only random happenstance that the sun rising above the mountains is so beautiful as to warrant the feeling of time standing still, yet presented right in front of you is the natural way we measure time — the movement of the sun across the Earth's horizon? Or is nature a design of some supreme power, whose infinite wisdom and infinite vision is responsible for producing such a mind-boggling landscape? Maybe the reason the desert is so comforting is because it is the latter.

The stillness, the isolation, the vastness, the untouched nature. This is what attracts me to the desert. I hope the reader gets to experience it at least once in their life.

**FOURTH WEEK OF OCTOBER, 2019:** This week saw me make one of the most condensed travel trips. On Tuesday night, I hopped in a plane to fly from Portland, Maine to Seattle, Washington. This was my third Seattle trip in four weeks.

I arrived in Seattle at about 8 p.m. local time and had my hearing with my client, Tim, at 8 a.m. the next day. He was a 75-year-old Navy veteran, who had a claim for PTSD. He was very conversational and entirely grateful for everything he had in his life. He had a smile that could light up a room, and demeanor that would make him a friend of anyone he met. I could see nothing ever getting him down, but boy was I proven wrong.

In the hearing Tim told the judge about his various in-service experiences. He was so engrossed in his story that he brought props. Purely for point of reference, he brought a picture of his wife, who has been his rock and who unfortunately, according to Tim, has had to live with his mood swings, suicidal tendencies, and other mental health symptoms. He also brought a picture of the submarine on which he proudly served for four years in the 1960s. He was responsible for relaying coded messages to the fire control station for the submarine's nuclear weapons. This heavy responsibility greatly impacted 19-year old Tim, who stated he "grew up" on that submarine. The pressure was so intense and reprieves few in number. Ever since his service, Tim had been dealing with feelings of guilt, pressure, and anxiety at the thought that he'd "had a hand" in preventing World War III by "never firing the missiles." The pressure — like that which inflicted my Philadelphia client, Peter — was crushing. He told the judge how he devotes his days to singing, even singing at scheduled engagements (these bring purpose to his life), and how he keeps himself surrounded by family.

At one point, however, he stated how his demons almost won. In 2012, he told his son very matter-of-factly that he was going to kill himself. He just couldn't handle the pressure, guilt, and anxiety even 50 years after service. Appalled, the son said, "Dad, I'm taking you down to the VA," and thus was the start of Tim's mental health treatment. He told this story without breaking up, as calmly as he told the judge and I about his singing. Throughout the whole 45 minute hearing, the judge was incredible. She was personable, inquisitive, and took a real interest in Tim's case. One could tell she appreciated Tim's "cute old man" disposition, as if she were reminded of her own father. As soon as the hearing was over, I had to run out to catch a flight. But Tim and I had a meaningful goodbye. He shook my hand and gripping my arm, said, "Tyler, I believe this is the beginning of a wonderful friendship." I hope I get to talk to him again. I felt bad rushing out so quickly, as I would have enjoyed getting to know him more, but my flight left in a mere hour and a half.

Therefore, I was in Seattle less than 15 hours before I hopped on a flight to take me back to the East Coast. My next destination was Newark, New Jersey, where I was born. This was the first time I had been to New Jersey for this job. Unfortunately, I only spent a mere matter of hours here, as well. I got into town around 9 p.m. Wednesday night and went directly over to the Meadowlands, where my hotel was located. My hearing was at 8:30 the next morning. I arrived early to find my client waiting for the building to open. He was a 76-year-old Vietnam veteran whose injuries stemmed from a Vietnam War gunshot wound to the right ankle. The veteran's daughter accompanied him. This hearing was notable because, to my surprise, it was an in-person hearing with a judge I had had before. (I only determined this for sure when the judge said she recognized my name.) This was only my third in-person hearing, and the first since June. I prefer these as it is easier to make a connection with the judge when you are right across the table.

Unfortunately, I learned in April 2020 that this veteran had died earlier that month, before a decision was rendered in his case. Therefore, his claims had to be dismissed for lack of Board of Veterans' Appeals jurisdiction. I called the daughter to offer my condolences. According to her lay opinion, her father literally worried himself to death over the COVID-19 situation. He was terrified to leave his house in the densely populated part of New Jersey where they lived.

I had to run out of this hearing, as well, as I jumped in a rental car and drove six and a half hours to Cleveland, Ohio, for the last two hearings of this massive travel swing. I felt bad I couldn't spend the day in New Jersey, visiting all the family-related sites I wanted to visit in Carteret, but I knew there would be another visit before long. The drive to Cleveland — which with the exception of only a couple hours was entirely from one end of Pennsylvania to another — was more scenic than I expected. The scenery was obviously post-peak foliage, but nonetheless, I enjoyed the drive amongst rolling hills and the red-tinted signs of autumn. I got into Cleveland around 5 p.m. and afforded myself a much-needed treadmill run, the first intensive exercise I had had since hiking in Big Bend National Park a week prior. The fact that the hotel provided free Texas Roadhouse for dinner capped a good day.

The next morning hearings went well, and as soon as I was done, I headed to the airport. My flight home arrived in Portland at 5 p.m. Therefore, in the space of three days (Tuesday night to Friday night), I flew from Portland to Seattle, Seattle to Newark, drove from Newark to Cleveland, and then flew from Cleveland to Portland. Incredible! During a Sunday night men's league hockey game, something I tried to attend as much as possible, I told a friend about this crazy trip. He was incredulous.

**FIFTH WEEK OF OCTOBER, 2019:** This week saw me take a neutered trip to Waco, Texas. I flew out on Monday, had hearings on Tuesday and Wednesday, and flew home Thursday. I flew into Dallas, rented a car, and drove an hour and a half to Waco, which I had last visited in July. The drive down was awful, however, because I flew into Dallas at night, in the rain, and drove along crowded, construction-filled I-35 to Waco. It was a stressful drive, but I was relieved to have resigned myself to staying in Waco for the couple days I was there, as Waco is not in the desert part of Texas, and therefore, it was unappealing for me to explore.

The hearings themselves were fairly unremarkable, and I was happy to fly home. I think I was exhausted from my previous week's travels, so I was looking forward to a more relaxed trip. Furthermore, I didn't feel like I was missing out on anything because I wasn't in an area of Texas that I was thrilled to go to. At this point in my travels — and particularly with the setting in of winter — I was OK with quick in-and-out trips if the hearing was in a previously-visited place.

# NOVEMBER 2019

———◆◆———

**FIRST WEEK OF NOVEMBER, 2019:** This week saw me take a day trip to Detroit and forgo a trip to Los Angeles and Phoenix later in the week.

My hearing in Detroit on Monday, November 4, 2019, was notable because this was the first time I flew into a place for a hearing and flew out the same day. My flight out of Portland started boarding at 4:56 a.m., and it landed in Detroit at 7:30 a.m. I had a few hours before I had to get over to the regional office for the 12:30 p.m. hearing, so I hung around the airport for a bit, had coffee, read, played a couple computer games, and then got a Lyft over to the regional office. I arrived at 11 a.m. and found lunch at a great hockey-themed place called The Anchor Bar. When it came time to go into the hearing, I learned why my co-workers said that the Detroit VA regional office has a reputation for working slowly. My client and I did not get into the hearing until 2:30 p.m.

My client, Johnny, bears mention. He was a 77-year-old Vietnam Army veteran. He served two years in Vietnam and had corresponding heart and mental health claims. He was very pleasant and conversational, but he spoke slowly, most likely the result of a stroke incurred 11 years prior. He was heavyset but had recently lost about 55 pounds. He walked deliberately and seemingly always appeared as if in a haze. He wasn't nonsensical, but it was obvious he either had some memory problems, cognitive problems, or a combination of the two. He stated his daughter thought he had dementia, which would not surprise me in the least. While in the waiting room, Johnny volunteered stories of his time in Vietnam, and he always

maintained a positive demeanor, smiling at me as if he was talking to one of
his grandkids. He was a helicopter mechanic who accompanied helicopter
crews on clean up operations. After a firefight the helicopter would come
in and take away bodies, pick up debris, and repair battle-worn equipment.
In his capacity he saw many dead bodies, saw friends die, and experienced
the terrors of a combat zone. While he was OK telling me about these
experiences in the waiting room, he simply and utterly broke down in the
hearing. It was heart-wrenching to see this sweet old man reduced to tears.
But the courage he displayed left a lasting impression on me.

Like in many hearings, I necessarily have to take veterans "back over there"
to Vietnam, Iraq, Germany, Korea — whenever they served. The judge
needs as holistic an understanding of a veteran's story as possible. So hearings were mostly devoted to veterans telling the judge what kind of service,
and what kind of horrors, they experienced "over there." I felt bad doing
it — reliving some of these memories was what many of these guys spent
most of their lives trying not to do — but it was necessary in order to present as sympathetic a case as possible to the judge. The double meaning as
applied to me going out around the country, always to come home again, is
why I thought *There and Back Again* was a perfect title for this book. Credit
to my brother and father for thinking of it.

Our hearing was the last of the day, so Johnny and I sat alone in the hearing
room for about 20 minutes after the hearing was over. He attempted to
compose himself many times. He sobbed through his tears, saying "I have
just tried to forget my whole life," and expressing that he was ashamed to
be crying about his Vietnam experiences, which he always tried to avoid
telling people about. He said only his wife knew he was in Vietnam, but
even she did not know the details that Johnny related to the judge and
me. I felt awful — here was a man tearfully trying to understand what has
happened to him and why he was feeling the way he did, reflecting on how
ill-treated he was when he returned from his Vietnam deployment. ("They
called us baby killers," is how he described his return to Los Angeles after
his deployment.) I tried my best to comfort him within the confines of
the professional relationship we had — but I am a lawyer, not a counselor.
I told him how pleased I was with how the hearing went and how I was

proud of him for testifying to his service. Johnny obviously had no awareness of PTSD or any of the symptoms he was experiencing, such as intense sadness, blocked memories, crying spells, etc. This only reinforced to me that one of the best things the VA does is not award retroactive benefits to veterans, but provide free healthcare and, importantly, mental health counseling. However, Johnny did not use any of these services.

After he composed himself, I walked him out to the lobby, where his daughter was slated to pick him up. When he got seated and settled, I leaned in close, shook his hand, and told him how fulfilling it was to help him today. He appreciated me being there. I arrived back at the airport at 4:30 p.m. and killed time waiting for my 8 p.m. flight home. A full day, for sure, but I was not anxious to again "commute" to the edge of the East Coast time zone anytime soon.

This trip was further notable because, upon leaving the Detroit airport to head to the hearing, I could say I had visited all 48 contiguous states over the course of my life. I was going to turn 27 years old in five months. I have an active competition going with College Bill — who has done a fair share of traveling over the course of his life — to see who will be the first to get to Alaska and Hawaii.

This week was supposed to see me leave on Wednesday to go to Los Angeles and Phoenix. However, on Tuesday night, November 5, 2019, I received a phone call from my father. My dad is not a talker — you would be hard-pressed to get two words out of him if you asked him his full name — so to get a call from him in any sense is unusual. He asked me if I was home. I said yes and told him, that night was one of the only days this week I would be in state. I had just settled down in my living room to track election results. He asked me if Catherine was there and if I could put him on speaker phone so both she and I could hear him. *Oh no*, I thought.

He said, "There is no easy way to say this, but Grandma is gone." I don't remember what he said after that. My heart sank. I don't believe I said anything for several minutes. I reoriented myself and told him Catherine and I would be home in an hour and a half. I threw my cell phone charger into my already-packed bag (I was supposed to leave for Los Angeles the next morning), picked up my sister-in-law who lived only a couple miles away, and drove up with them to Freedom, where we met my parents, brother, and life-long friend, Mitch, who was with my brother when my dad called him.

When we arrived in Freedom, we all sat around the dining room table. My dad explained what happened and the instantaneous nature of Grandma's death. We all assumed a massive heart attack took her as she had been coping with severe heart and vascular problems for the past couple of years.

The thought of leaving the next morning to go spend the next four days by myself was almost unbearable. But I resolved that night that I was going to attend the Los Angeles hearing as planned. That's what Grandma would have wanted. My sickening heartbreak and shock did not outweigh the interest my clients had in having their hearings. They had waited too long and were in much more unfortunate situations than I.

Catherine and I left Freedom on Wednesday morning, and I had to stop at the office before flying to Los Angeles. I arrived, probably looking like I had only a couple hours of sleep, with everything else but work on my mind.

I will never forget the way my co-workers pulled together to help me in that time of need. I told Janet, the office manager, why I was late getting into the office. She sprung into action. She got together with others and made my life so much easier. Within a half hour we had a plan. My co-worker, Kirsten, stayed in Phoenix for my Friday hearing (thankfully he was already there for a conference), and another co-worker, Jordan, went to Los Angeles for me. A short-notice plane ticket from Maine to Los Angeles was surely a considerable expense! Co-worker Tori took my client calls for the rest of the week, and I was able to turn around and go back to Freedom, where I spent Wednesday through Monday afternoon.

Much like the response the Freedom community had to my family's time of need, I will forever be grateful for the generosity exhibited by the firm in accommodating me this way. My co-workers allowed me to grieve with my family in the aftermath of the biggest shock any of us had ever faced. I inquired later whether the firm wanted me to reimburse them for the flights I had already booked to go to Los Angeles and Phoenix. I received a call from Jack a couple days later, expressing his condolences and telling me not to worry about the wasted plane tickets. These were the only flights I ever missed traveling for Jackson and MacNichol.

**SECOND WEEK OF NOVEMBER, 2019:** My spirits low, I traveled on Monday afternoon to New Orleans for a hearing Tuesday morning, and then traveled to Indianapolis for a hastily scheduled hearing for Wednesday. I was supposed to get into New Orleans on Monday night, but I stuck around Freedom on Monday for the Veterans Day celebration, for which I was still the master of ceremonies despite Grandma's death. However, bad weather in the connecting airport of Detroit meant I missed my Atlanta–New Orleans flight. I therefore spent the night in the Atlanta airport — a much more comfortable experience than the time I spent the night in the Charlotte airport. I was able to stretch out on a grouping of chairs and catch a flight that got me into New Orleans at 8:45 a.m. I was not so agitated as when I almost missed my friends' wedding. This Delta flight was cancelled because of the weather, not by anything in Delta's control, like airplane maintenance. I wrote this poem about this overnight stay, and called it "Scenes from Gate A4."

*I arrive late*
*Tired, worn, and sore.*
*I'm curled up at gate A4.*

*I'm going to miss my flight,*
*Spend the night in this place.*
*Not so for the lady*
*getting red in the face.*

*A family of four bedded down,*
*Claiming their land like a little shanty town*
*The snow batters the windows; it's cold on the bench.*

*No places open, no room to stretch.*
*My backpack's a pillow, suit jacket a cover;*
*Another night spent without my partner.*

*Three hours go by with rotten sleep,*
*But then the sun starts to peak, so I'm back on my feet.*
*Run to the next terminal, stick to the plan.*
*Here we go all over again.*
*Janitor's pushing his livelihood around the floor,*
*Taking an early morning tour of gate A4.*

My hearing was scheduled for 8:30 but was running late, such that I arrived at the regional office in time. Two hours later I was back in a Lyft heading back to the New Orleans airport. I then caught my Indianapolis flight no problem. I had no time to stick around New Orleans and explore it further, as was my desire after my visit there in July.

The Indianapolis hearing was somewhat unusual as the lead testifier was the veteran's wife. She did most of the talking and stuck to relevant points in a concise, sympathy-provoking manner. My presentation was facilitated by Tori's excellent note-taking, as this was one of the calls I would have taken if I wasn't back in Freedom grieving with my family. The client was first on the docket, leading us to adjourn the hearing in more than enough time for me to get back to the airport and arrive home in Portland around 3 p.m.

This week necessarily saw me spend my first nights alone after Grandma's death. At this point, I truly think it had not hit me yet. At the time I wrote that I didn't know how to describe how I felt regarding her death. I was heartbroken, for sure. Even now, I am most sad that Catherine will never get to know her beyond the year and a half she did. I will always be comforted by the intense love and affection she showed my wife, who she called "My Catherine."

When I was alone during my travels, I found my coping mechanism was trying to keep myself distracted from my own thoughts. Sleep afforded relief, as did Netflix, Hulu, Steam (the computer game platform) — anything to keep me occupied, if not busy. I started taking my personal laptop on the road with me, as the introduction of cold weather throughout the country meant I could not get out and do the outdoorsy things I would normally do when I traveled for work. I also started falling asleep at night listening to replays of shows on Sirius XM's POTUS channel. All this made my times away from home better, but my sadness and grief combined with the cold weather made for a very tough fall.

My Indianapolis client said something for which I am thankful. I apologized for being unusually unprepared without written material because it had been a roller coaster of a week, starting with my grandmother's death. He said, "Oh, I'm so sorry for your loss . . . I never knew my grandmother." That made me realize how lucky I was to know her and to be mutually involved in each other's lives as much as we were. For sure her values, spirits, and memories will live on in all of us. I will never be so unfortunate to ever say, "I never knew my grandmother."

The latter half of the week saw me travel to Jackson, Mississippi, on Thursday afternoon and return Friday afternoon. This trip was super short and condensed — I flew on six different flights over the course of the 24-hour period. For some odd reason, it is very difficult to get to Jackson from Portland. Luckily, I was able to catch my 10:30 a.m. flight home after telling the Jackson hearing coordinator that I was unavoidably pressed for time. I arrived home around 7:30 p.m. and was able to get up to Brunswick to have a much-needed poker night with my three best law school friends.

**FOURTH WEEK OF NOVEMBER, 2019:** This week saw me drive down to New Jersey for a hearing in Newark, my second such hearing and the first time in a while I was able to add to my map a new place or traveling route. The drive was quite bearable because of the fantastic rental car I had. This was the trip I planned on taking my grandmother on, so it was bittersweet to go to New Jersey without her. The last time I drove down to New Jersey was when I went with her in September 2018. My family comes from New Jersey, and my grandmother lived in the same town for

60 years before moving to Maine. She would have loved to accompany me on this trip.

The trip was very smooth, both there and back. I went over the George Washington Bridge, drove on the Jersey Turnpike, and got into and out of Newark just fine. I was thrilled to get on the road again after spending so much time on planes. At the same time, I was thrilled that when I wrote this journal entry, I was not slated to have another hearing until December 5, and the next time I was to get on a plane was scheduled for December 18.

This trip ended the fall section of this travel journal. Overall, I think there are a few obvious lessons: The honeymoon phase of this travel job was over, yet at the same time the job was as fulfilling as ever, at least when it came to client relationships and effectively helping people. There were a few quite notable moments in travel, such as visiting Texas again, but I had started going back to the same places for hearings, and therefore, I was exposing myself to less diverse travel locations. I started prioritizing spending more time at home, which was leading me to spend less time out of state. I definitely grew weary of airplanes and airports much more easily and got very anxious when flights were delayed, like when I was coming home from Jackson and I feared being prohibitively late to the poker night I had planned. I found myself looking at job postings in state government and daydreaming about actually having a normal work schedule. However, I still loved the type of legal work I did. I really enjoyed the balance between oral advocacy and persuasive writing. I still found it hard to believe that I was actually able to accomplish my goal of passing the bar and that I was a full-fledged attorney at a law firm.

WINTER

# DECEMBER 2019

———— ◆◆ ————

**FIRST WEEK OF DECEMBER, 2019:** Nicely, I had a two-week time period free from hearing travel. I still had to work, but I did not need to go anywhere but the office. This was a *wonderful* respite. I enjoyed being home and with Catherine. I saw my friends and family and got to actually drive my own car places! I made many trips to Freedom, which was also a nice break from the normal. Overall, I had November 20 to December 4 free from travel. On December 4, I drove eight-and-a-half hours to Lebanon, Pennsylvania, for a hearing I had scheduled for December 5. I looked forward to the driving as opposed to flying. I really needed a break from flying. While driving, you can be more of a master of your own destiny. I get so fed up with flight delays and circumstances outside my control. At least in a car I can decide when to stop, where to stop, and could leave Portland whenever I wanted.

The drive itself was long. I did not get a good night's sleep the previous night, so I struggled to stay awake for most of the drive. I kept busy listening to Sirius XM and Spotify. Despite my normal high tolerance for long road trips, on this trip I found myself stopping more often than normal in order to stretch my legs and get something to eat.

**SECOND WEEK OF DECEMBER 2019:** This week saw me travel again to Newark, New Jersey. This was a much more bearable drive than the one the previous week due to it being only six hours. Growing up I thought a drive to New Jersey was unbearably long — now it is no big deal! I stopped at the same Subway and Dunkin' donuts rest area in Connecticut as I did on my trip to Lebanon and my first trip to Newark. I used the time to listen to President Trump's impeachment proceedings on Sirius XM and had an almost hour-long conversation with Grandad. I stayed at the same Linden, New Jersey, Hampton Inn as I did the first time I was there.

Grandad loved hearing about my work. Our conversations would typically last at least an hour. I would take down time in an airport, or a boring stretch of a long drive, and call him. He loved hearing about where I was, what I thought of the place, and my various clients. He was always interested in what branch of the service they were in and what kind of disabilities they had. He never could say enough how proud he was of me.

The two hearings in Newark went well. This was the first time where I had clients who were in their 30s. In fact, both were only 10 years older than me, and both were completely unemployable because of their already service-connected mental health conditions, among other issues. Interestingly, they both were deployed to Iraq and witnessed suicide bombings. When they came home, they had trouble processing their emotions and felt like they were abandoned by the Army. One guy lost a girlfriend and had to move in with his parents, who tried in every possible way to help him deal with the effects of his PTSD.

It's sobering to have clients who were not much older than me. These clients were so much more different than previous clients because, quite frankly, many of my clients are Vietnam veterans who are advanced in age. These two guys in Newark had their whole lives ahead of them. I felt increased pressure to make sure I could make these guys as financially well off as possible, so they could focus on getting the mental health treatment they needed.

Both cases were huge successes. We had a judge as favorable as the judge I mentioned in my Wyoming hearing. He did not take long to render his decision, granting all the benefits we sought in both cases.

The drive back home was uneventful, but it made me realize that I have no desire to do *another* New England or mid-Atlantic drive anytime soon.

**THIRD WEEK OF DECEMBER, 2019:** This week saw me go to Waco on Sunday, Newark *again* on Tuesday, home for a brief time on Wednesday night/Thursday morning, and then back to Waco on Thursday afternoon!

I must admit, I was looking forward to getting back on the road — and specifically to places requiring air travel — after my almost month-long reprieve. I enjoyed getting back to my airplane routine and earning those airline points despite the plane fatigue I felt in late November and early December.

It took three flights to get to Dallas, and then I had an hour-and-a-half car ride from Dallas to Waco. My hearing on Monday morning was in front of a judge I have grown to really like, but the hearing was a bit too disjointed for my taste after the judge brought up a few issues that might have been withdrawn and that were therefore not on my preparatory sheet. However, I conveyed all the relevant points I wanted and traveled back to Dallas that afternoon in order to spend Monday night in Dallas. For the first time in quite a few weeks, I felt energized to explore, meet new people, and discover new places.

Therefore, I decided to venture back out into the part of Dallas' downtown called Deep Ellum, where College Bill and I spent the night during our July Dallas visit. I wanted to go back to St. Pete's Dancing Marlin. As I had lyrically memorialized his story and the restaurant, I wanted to see if our old waiter, Gino, still worked there. I also wanted to either explore a new piano bar or go back to Louie Louie's Piano Bar.

I arrived in town around 4 p.m. and walked the mile from my hotel to Deep Ellum. Sure enough, right when I walked into St. Pete's I saw Gino. I didn't think I would recognize him, but as soon as I saw his scrawny figure I knew it was him. Not wanting to act like a total creeper, I posted up at the bar, where the bartender took my order. I pretended to barely remember Gino's name and asked the bartender if he still worked here. The bartender said he did and that she would tell him that there was someone here to say hi.

When he came over, I assured him that I had no expectation that he would remember me, never mind my name. I told him I remembered him because this was a memorable place, his story stuck with me (how he left home in Michigan without telling anyone and made a new life for himself down here), and that I appreciated it when he told Bill and I we were the kind of customers that made his job fun. It took him a couple minutes to jog his memory, but he asserted he did remember that conversation. He was moved that I not only remembered him, but that I took the time to reintroduce myself. Gino couldn't stick around for long as he had to keep moving between his tables. But we chatted for a couple minutes each time he would swing by my part of the bar. I told him I still did the job I did back in July, that I really enjoyed coming to Dallas, and that my job frequently took me to Waco.

I asked the bartender where I should go next, as I was trying to kill about an hour and half before 8 p.m. when Louie Louie's opened. She recommended a New Orleans-inspired Cajun place next door, called The Free Man, where live music was expected that night. I went over, and I was the only one in the restaurant besides the bartender and a customer named Ed, who worked for Southwest and, I learned, was one of the owners of the place. Hopefully, Monday nights were not their busiest! I chatted with Ed for a while, but I wanted to stretch my legs before The Free Man's live music started at 7:30 p.m. I walked around and found an ice cream place. I passed a very steam-punk-looking alley, called Radiator Alley, which connected one street to another. I saw some shady figures. Not many people were out at that relatively early hour on a weekday.

I walked around the block and made my way back to The Free Man. I sat for about 30 minutes, listening to the jazzy foursome playing in the corner of the bar. The keyboardist was the standout player and was actually from New Brunswick, which borders eastern Maine. The other three were a bass player, guitar player, and drummer. Surprisingly, I was not up for staying out until 9 p.m., when Louie's music would start up, so I walked back to my hotel. I had to get up early for my flight to Newark.

I was really thrilled with my visit to Dallas. I didn't do much, but I felt like I broke out of my couple-month slump and was actually excited to get out and explore again. I think this revitalization was due to my lack of travel over the past couple weeks, therefore denying me of the opportunity to explore new places and meet new people. I wrote a poem on the way home called "Deep Ellum Revisited."

*Trade 20 degrees for 90,*
*Everything looks the same.*
*Saw Gino at St. Pete's*
*Still Bussing Tables Everyday.*

*The City is Alive.*
*It's a cold, cold, winter day.*
*The Free Man's got music at 7:30,*
*But Louie Louie's isn't open that early.*

*Radiator Alley's got an art deco feel*
*While scantily clad girls smoke and adjust their high heels.*
*You can get there by scooter, by foot, or by car;*
*I can't wait to visit this particular bar.*

*Post up, Nichole says, "Hey where've you been?"*
*Heavy sign in response, "Just pour me a gin."*
*She furrows her brow, says no need to be solemn.*
*Music plays, people sway, down here in Deep Ellum.*

The flight to Newark on Tuesday morning/afternoon was not fun because I was fighting off a cold. But I got that hearing done in time to catch my flight home to Maine. It was the first time I had flown United back to Maine. I arrived home at 3 p.m., happy to spend an evening with Catherine. I even got to spend some time with her for lunch the next day before departing to go back to Waco. That's right — two Waco trips in one week!

It's telling that when I left for Waco on Thursday afternoon, I purposely left on an afternoon flight, not a morning flight. Such were my continued attempts to start spending as much time as possible at home. My flight out of Portland was delayed, so much so that I was going to get into Dallas at 9 p.m. So I elected to stay in Dallas that night, having left that town only three days prior, and then drive to Waco on Friday morning. I completed this drive easily and stopped on the way in West, Texas. I wanted to check out their famous Czech and Eastern European-focused downtown area. My goal was to stop in one of the antique shops and see if there was something I could get Catherine for Christmas. I stopped in a shop that had just opened and was staffed by an old cowboy with the heaviest Texas accent I had ever heard. Everything in the store was dusty and from his personal collection. I must have looked severely out of place wearing my suit. I was unsuccessful in finding something for Catherine, but nevertheless, I found interest in checking out this seemingly out-of-place town. At the very least it killed time for me, as I was otherwise going to get into Waco a couple hours earlier than I needed to.

I had my 12:30 p.m. hearing in Waco on time, begged the hearing coordinator to go first on the docket given my tight schedule, and left Waco in time to get to my 4 p.m. plane out of Dallas. This was a major victory for me as I thought for sure that I was going to miss my 4 p.m. flight. The hearing started at 12:45, we were done by 1:30, and I got back to Dallas with about an hour to spare. Incredibly, I arrived home in Portland on time, around 11:40 p.m. I was immensely pleased because I had easily foreseen end-of-the-week difficulties, like plane maintenance or getting delayed because of something like the flight crew clocking out. But Delta came through for me, and I was able to start my Christmas-New Years break off right. I started a break where I would not leave the state again until January 6.

# JANUARY 2020

——◆◆——

**SECOND WEEK OF JANUARY, 2020:** This week saw me leave for a January 7 hearing in St. Paul, Minnesota. I had an unremarkable flight out and got into St. Paul around 5 p.m. that night. This was my first time in St. Paul since my very first hearing on June 6, 2019. I went to a place called Amsterdam Bar and Grill, a little hipster bar with two music stages. There was no live music that night, and the place was not really crowded. There were two college-age girls sitting to my left talking sports and a couple at the other end of the bar having a fierce argument with the guy obviously drunk and "quite a few shots in" according to the bartender. Surprisingly, there was an older grandmotherly type to my right, and various other people scattered around the square-shaped bar. The cantina scene from *Star Wars* came to mind. Near the end of my meal I awkwardly injected myself into the ladies' football conversation. No one ever said I was a ladies' man.

On my way back to my hotel I passed the Eagle Bar and Grill, which was attached to the Hampton Inn. I went in and was literally the only person there. I forced myself to have a beer and made idle chitchat with the bartender. We talked about how the Minnesota Vikings had just won their big playoff game on Sunday, in overtime against the New Orleans Saints. The bartender was born, raised, and currently lived in St. Paul. I finished my drink fairly quickly and was surprised to see it was only 6:30 p.m. I went back to my hotel and did some work before heading to bed. I also spoke with Grandad for about 40 minutes. I sent him my law journal article about hearing cancellations, the one inspired by the June 2019 cancelled hearing I'd had in Huntington, West Virginia. He thoroughly enjoyed reading my article, as well as the others in that journal's edition.

The next morning, I worked in the hotel room before heading to my hearing. At that time, I received a call from the office, where I was informed that the VA DC regional office, where the judges sat for these virtual hearings, was going to close in about an hour. Therefore, I had to rush over to the VA to try and get in my hearing. Otherwise, it was going to be cancelled! I skipped the early lunch I was getting ready for and hustled over to the VA regional office. I met with the client, who thankfully was there already, but we ended up being too late. The judge did not want to start a hearing only 20 minutes before the VA was going to close. Obviously, both my client and I were extremely disappointed, but I made sure to note to him and the hearing coordinator that this cancellation was really no one's fault. Apparently, Washington DC, where the VA was headquartered, was facing flash flood warnings. The unpredictable nature of such a natural phenomenon meant that no reasonable notice could be given to me or my client, making this situation far different from my June 2019 hearing cancellation incident.

This particular client had a rough path to his Board of Veterans' Appeals hearing. This January hearing was cancelled and rescheduled for March 20. This March hearing was cancelled due to the COVID-19 pandemic. The hearing was rescheduled for June. In May 2020, I saw in the internal VA system that this hearing was postponed as well! I quickly contacted the St. Paul VA hearing coordinator and respectfully inquired why this upcoming hearing was already postponed. I'm so glad I did, as the hearing coordinator figured out that the hearing was postponed in error and that we could actually have a hearing in early June. I was able to represent the client in this hearing, a nice full circle from going out to St. Paul in January to represent him the first time around.

On Wednesday I flew to New Jersey for my fourth hearing in Newark over the past two months. This time, however, I did not stay in Linden, but in a Hampton Inn in Newark, on the east side of the Passaic River. I did this because I wanted a change of pace, and my hearing was at 8:30 a.m. Jersey traffic is notorious, so I didn't want to take any chances of not making it to the hearing in time. This change of location was a great choice, and I will do it every time I go to Newark. I stayed in a room with a great view of the city and went to dinner at a diner three blocks down the street, called Tops Diner. It is apparently one of the best diners in the country. The menu was probably close to 15 pages long, and the restaurant had a great 1950s feel. Grandma would have loved it. I highly enjoyed my meal there, and I further enjoyed the fact that it was only a couple blocks from my hotel. In the morning, I walked over to the Federal Building.

My client might as well have introduced himself as "Tony from the Bronx." A heavy-set, "What-ya-goin-do-about-it" kind of guy who walked into his hearing straight off the set of the *Sopranos*, it didn't take much for me to believe he was born and raised in New York City but now lived on the Jersey Shore. A leather jacket and Yankees cap completed his central casting costume call. His hearing regarded individual unemployability based on his severe depression. In other words, we were trying to prove to the VA that he was incapable of "seeking or maintaining" gainful employment because of his depression, which the VA already conceded was due to his military service. Unexpectedly, he got emotional at how his post-service depression had almost ruined his life. He has self-isolated from friends and family, and could not focus on work enough to remain employed. As he was telling the judge how his depression was like a "dark cloud" over his life, his face scrunched up and tears started flowing down his face. He apologized but stayed emotional. Struggling to speak on how he has to navigate life through the omnipresent lens of depression, he exasperatedly said, "I feel like an invisible man!" I was on the verge of tears myself; the judge was visibly moved. The resulting silence said more than words could. Waiting in the airport on the way home, I jotted down this poem and called it "An Invisible Man":

*Rain falls on a dreary city;*
*A fog completes my endless pity.*
*I came home from Nam in '75*
*Forty years ain't enough to turn the tide.*

*No kids, no wife, living's a chore.*
*My life seems empty here on the Shore.*
*I served my country, what, for this?*
*I wish the rain for once, would miss.*

*I am an Invisible Man.*
*I soldier on as only soldiers can.*
*Saunter through this world, waiting to die,*
*Death's no fear if you're never alive.*

*I am an Invisible Man,*
*Forsaken by country, that was not the plan.*
*My soul's afflicted with invisible wounds;*
*I stand here alone, not knowing what to do.*
*I saunter through this world, waiting to die;*
*Death's no fear if you're never alive.*

In May 2020, I was so excited to learn that the judge did exactly what I asked him to do — granted Tony 100 percent compensation, effective to January 1, 2012. This was one of the most successful cases I had, netting the client almost $130,000. In my excitement, it was only after Tony's phone starting ringing that I realized I was calling at 7:30 in the morning. When he picked up, I apologized for calling so early, but I wanted to deliver some great news. I told him the judge's decision. He gasped and said, "Oh man, you can call me at 1 o'clock in the morning with news like that!" In his thick New Yorker accent, he described how he was losing hope on this case and had thought the time the judge was taking in issuing a decision was indicative of a poor result. I assured him otherwise and congratulated him on the judge's decision. On a personal note, I thanked him for the opportunity to represent him and for his service to our country.

Even to the present day, these kinds of calls are my favorite part of my job. Nothing is more fulfilling than hearing a client's relief at a favorable result.

**THIRD WEEK OF JANUARY, 2020:** This week saw me make a day trip to Detroit, my first one since November. This trip was fairly unremarkable.

I hung out exclusively in the Detroit airport, reading, watching Hulu, or learning German on Duolingo. Despite the monotony, the time passed quickly. I left home at 3:57 a.m. and returned at 10:40 p.m. This trip ended the holiday lull of little-traveling.

**FOURTH WEEK OF JANUARY, 2020:** On Monday, Martin Luther King's birthday, I left for San Diego, where I was to remain through Wednesday morning. I was excited because this was the first time in quite a few months that I went to a city I had not been to before. I arrived in San Diego around 11 a.m. Monday morning and went to the USS *Midway* museum ship.

This was a fascinating experience. Despite reading about aircraft carriers all my life, I believe this was the first time I had actually seen one in person, never mind got to go on one. The *Midway* served from 1945 to 1992. It held 4,500 crew and was deployed through the Pacific, finally being retired after Operation Desert Shield in 1991. I was fascinated to learn that the ship consumed 292 gallons of fuel per mile.

Being inside a carrier was eye-opening. The conditions these men lived in were appalling. I took several pictures of the enlisted men's cots, where they were expected to live and work in such cramped conditions. Exposed electrical wire lined the ship; the engine room seemed like one big death trap. The ship also had several real-life models of the various kinds of aircraft that served on the Midway throughout her life. I took a picture of a Corsair, my paternal grandfather's favorite fighter. He was a Navy veteran. I found myself thinking of him throughout my tour of the ship. While he did not serve on an aircraft carrier, he did serve in the engine room of a ship in the 1950s, and therefore, I thought I got an adequate glimpse into what his kind of living and work situation was like the two years he was in the Navy. Across the bow of the *Midway*, I could look out over the harbor and see the recently arrived USS *Abraham Lincoln*, which had just docked that morning after spending a record-breaking 294 days at sea.

I wanted to tour the ship because of my general interest in American military history, but I left thinking more about how I could help my Navy clients more constructively develop theories of their cases. I felt like I could somewhat empathize with clients when they would tell me how awful or anxiety-producing their lifestyles were on ships at sea. I could also see now why liberty on shore was so coveted by shipboard crew members.

That night I went to a bar called Bar One, which I originally was going to skip after having dinner. I am very glad I did not. I posted myself at the bar and started talking to the guy next to me. His name was Dave, and he physically recoiled when I told him I was a veterans' disability attorney. He told me he had just received his VA denial letter the day before. He proceeded to tell me about how he was stationed in Hawaii, had served 20 years, but was looking for a change for him and his family. But he was encountering issues with the VA. I actually did very little talking over the half an hour or 45 minutes we sat together. Instead, I got the sense he needed to vent a little to someone who could understand what kind of difficulty the VA was giving him. I left very proud of myself for staying out just a little longer despite my desire to go back to my hotel room, and in spite of my desire to not spend so much money. The cocktail I got at Bar One cost 15 dollars, but I am confident I will remember my conversation more with Dave than I will the tab at the end of the night.

The next day I had my hearing with a client named Chris. This client was notable not necessarily for his military story, but because of the conversation we had while we sat together for two and a half hours in the waiting room. He was in his early 50s, a police officer, and served in the Army for a few years in the 1990s. However, we talked primarily of my upcoming marriage, and he offered his advice on how to make a woman feel appreciated. He talked of how he believed in understanding your partner's love language, *i.e.* being sensitive to her needs and wants, etc. He related his thoughts because he recently went through divorce proceedings with his wife, but through learning about these relationship intricacies, he got his marriage back on track. I realized that beyond their military experience, my clients came from all different backgrounds and carried many life lessons due to their diverse experiences.

After the hearing, I booked it to El Cajon Mountain, about half an hour away from the VA regional office. This mountain is reputed to be the hardest and highest in the San Diego area. It was rated as the hardest on All-Trails and allegedly should have taken me around eight hours. It took me four. It was great to get back out on a mountain. I had not been on a hike since October, so I was eager to get out and get this exercise again. Unfortunately, the mountain did not deliver the kind of fantastic weather for which San Diego is known. Instead, a thick coat of fog enveloped the mountain. Occasionally, the sun would poke through and afford me a decent picture, but otherwise I hiked entirely in fog. But if one is to go on a hike purely for the exercise, this hike was ideal. It was about 60 degrees, with no wind, rain, or beating sun. On the way up the mountain I listened to James Taylor — a favorite artist to listen to when I'm out in peaceful nature.

When I got to the top, I sat to rest, rehydrate, and eat a couple of the protein bars I had brought along. Shortly after I settled down a guy came along. He seemed around my age. His name was Eddie, and incredibly, he was from Massachusetts and had just recently moved to San Diego. He was looking for a change in his life. He was tired of the New England weather and decided to make a change. He had been living in San Diego for only a couple months. He was a bartender but was looking to do something with his graduate degree in mental health counseling. We sat at the top of the mountain, just the two of us enveloped in thick white fog. Again, such a small, small world. I envied his sense of adventure and, like Gino in Dallas, his willingness to pick up and try to make a life for himself.

I really enjoyed my visit to San Diego. I was half-expecting an experience like Los Angeles, but such was not the case. I found I was able to walk around portions of the downtown area without fear or anxiety. The little I drove was free of heavy traffic. Food and drinks were expensive, but such is California. I was also thrilled to get a second wind and enjoy traveling for work again. I hoped this second wind would stick around for February, the month in which I would be home very little.

On Wednesday, I left for Jackson, Mississippi. I had two hearings that went well. I got to know the hearing coordinator, Marie, and the judge for both hearings, George Senyk. The judge and I bonded over the fact that both our last names were Ukrainian.

The morning of the hearings, I watched the series premiere of *Star Trek: Picard*. Ask any of my friends, and the first thing they will tell you about me is that I am a life-long, die-hard *Star Trek* fan. Watching the series premiere alone was very difficult. Usually, I would go over to Kyle's, and we would watch together. For this premiere, my parents and Mariah's parents came to Kyle and Mariah's house to all watch together. It killed me to miss this family gathering. But my absence was unavoidable, as was my absence for most of the Thursdays on which the show would air. *What am I going to do*, I asked myself, *ask the office to not send me anywhere Thursday nights or Friday mornings, just because I want to watch a TV show?* I realized the equities balanced in favor of me continuing my job unimpaired by the guilt I felt at missing watching this show with my family.

After the hearings, I left to make my way to Nashville, where I had a hearing scheduled for Friday afternoon. However, my Jackson hearings got done earlier than I expected, so I decided to spend Thursday night in Memphis, three hours away, and then make the final three-hour drive to Nashville on Friday morning. I was enthralled with the idea of experiencing Memphis' well-known downtown scene — the home of blues music! Since I had the time, I traveled to Memphis via Tupelo, Mississippi. I know the town from my Civil War studies, as well as the fact that it is Elvis Presley's hometown.

My decision to go to Memphis turned out to be a fantastic decision. I arrived in town around 5:30 p.m. and immediately went out into town. My hotel was only a block away from the beginning of Beale Street, the hub of downtown nightlife. This street was incredible. Bright lights filled the streets like Times Square. So many blues bars tried to attract business on what appeared to be a slow Thursday night. Blues and rock and roll filled the air — a house party at the heart of Memphis. This area reminded me of Fourth Street Live, the lively downtown section of Louisville, Kentucky, I visited in December 2017.

I was very excited to find a good house band and have dinner. I decided to duck into BB King's Blues Club, the original in a chain that has spread across the country. This restaurant had a house band that started playing 15 minutes after I arrived. The band lacked back-up singers or a powerful horn section, so it fell short of reminding me of the incredible blues band Bill and I watched at Louie Louie's Piano Bar in Dallas. But they were still very talented and fun to watch.

I left this bar at 7 p.m., looking for another place to broaden my experience in town. I went to a bar called Rum Boogie Café, which had a live band consisting of a few players. Again, this was not the kind of live band I was looking for. I posted up at the bar and started making conversation with a guy, whose name I did not get despite him telling me twice. I was shocked to learn he was from New Hampshire, and his father's family was from Fryeburg, Maine. Such a small world — I go to all these different places and only meet people from New England! We learned that he and I shared many similar interests. We talked *Star Wars*, *Star Trek*, the bars I like in Dallas, and the Blues Brothers. I only left when a coworker of his arrived. He worked for some sort of telecommunication company. He was visibly moved when I told him what I did for a living. When we parted and I shook his hand, he told me to "keep doing the good work." This was only further reinforcement of the love for my job.

I ended the night at a third place, King Jerry Lawler's Hall of Fame Bar and Grill. It's rare for me to stay out for a few hours in a downtown setting — indicative of how much I was enjoying the scene. This third bar had probably the most impressive-sounding house band. It was only a piano player, drummer, guitar player, and a singer. The singer sat next to me at the bar after his set. He said he had been friends with all those players for years. No doubt this contributed to their sound's tightness.

I returned to my hotel room at around 9 p.m., thoroughly satisfied with my first visit to Memphis.

Shortly before I arrived in Memphis, I received an email from the office saying my Friday afternoon hearing in Nashville was cancelled. I attempted to rebook my flight home, but there were no flights available. I therefore had all of Friday, until 5 p.m., to do what I wanted. I decided to leave Memphis early in the morning and proceeded the three and a half hours to Murfreesboro, Tennessee, about half an hour south of Nashville. Here was the Stones River National Battlefield, the site of a Civil War battle that took place over the course of the 1862-1863 New Year. I had visited this battlefield with my father in 2007, so for all intents and purposes, I did not remember it but for one particular monument that stuck in my mind, due to the monument's ironic proximity to a factory.

I arrived at the battlefield at 10 a.m. and quickly learned that the walking loop around the battlefield was only about three miles. I was itching to get some physical exercise, so I ran my way around the loop trail, stopping at the points of interest along the way. Unfortunately, there were only six tour stops, a sign that the battlefield was not very well preserved. I highly enjoyed this jaunt around the battlefield. The weather cleared, so that it seemed like a perfect Maine spring day. It was only partly cloudy and about 50 degrees. I was comfortable running around in a T-shirt and work-out shorts.

It only took me two hours to go through the battlefield and grab lunch at a nearby Subway. I decided to get to the Nashville airport early, so I spent a couple hours in the airport before my flight back to Portland. During this time, Catherine and I finalized our offer on the house in which we currently lived.

This week exemplified the mixed feelings I had whenever I was on the road. I enjoyed the adventure, but I missed Catherine terribly. Part of me thought that I should be with her, and it felt that while I was on the road, we were living separate lives. I suppose this issue would be remedied by work trips that were not an entire week in duration, but such trips were necessary sometimes. I had no idea that my travels were soon coming to an abrupt end.

The other side of me said, and remains convinced, that this was the time to do this travel. I would miss doing this job when I moved on to something else, so I should live it up now. Such had been my philosophy ever since I started this job. Sometimes, though, there were cracks in my conviction that were only remedied by a restorative stay at home. Part of me dreaded the upcoming February, when I was scheduled to be in Maine for only a few days out of the whole month. I knew I would truly miss my friends, family, and Catherine so, so much. As much as a part of me would miss the travel when I moved on to something else, the other part of me would be excited when I would be able to see the people I wanted to see without consideration of work travel. Reviewing this entry in August 2020, I fully endorse the thoughts I had this fourth week of January.

**FIFTH WEEK OF JANUARY, 2020:** This week saw me travel to Houston, Texas, for three days, as well as to Montgomery, Alabama, for a hearing.

Houston is a much more sprawled out city than I realized. I got my hotel in what I thought was the outside of the city, but it was way more hustling around the hotel than I wanted. I arrived in town around 7 p.m., and grabbed a quick chicken burger at a place called the Hopdoddy Burger Bar. It was a short walk from the hotel. Nicely though, that night I had an hour-long phone call with College Bill, only the second time I had spoken with him over the past couple months. We spent most of our conversation brainstorming our annual road trip, which as of this writing was going to center around a May 1 hearing I had scheduled in Phoenix. This plan, like literally everyone else's travel plans after mid-March, was obliterated due to COVID.

The next day I woke up with a head cold. Incredibly, this was the first time I had gotten sick while on the road. I think this sickness came about because I had only a couple hours of sleep the night before I left for Houston. I spent Monday after my hearing nursing myself. I drank plenty of water and did work on my work computer. I went for a couple mile walk around an arboretum nearby, but otherwise lay low in the hotel. It was a nice day — 70 degrees and partly cloudy, so I wanted to afford myself at least some opportunity to go outside.

The next day my hearing started exactly on time, 8:30 a.m. Therefore, I went back to the hotel after the hearing to take a quick nap. That nap, plus me loading up on orange juice in the morning, made me feel well enough to visit an exciting place, the Johnson Space Center, about 30 minutes outside of Houston.

Johnson Space Center is a college campus-like center dedicated to helping run the International Space Station (ISS), as well as research and development on many different kinds of probes and the United States' attempt to one day land a man on Mars. The actual visitor center is called Space Center Houston, and part of the visitor center experience involved taking a tram tour of Johnson Space Center. This space center was not as big as the Kennedy Space Center I visited in Florida, but it was fascinating nonetheless. There were exhibits dedicated to explaining how different systems on the ISS works, humanity's attempts to get to Mars, and the history of NASA's various manned space programs. Noteworthy was actually touching a real moon rock, chiseled down to a smooth, flat surface due to all the times it has been touched. The tram tour of the Johnson Space Center was also outstanding. I got to see the only surviving Apollo rocket, cannibalized from parts of the cancelled Apollo 18, 19, and 20 missions. This was the only example of an Apollo rocket replica that had original parts.

I also saw the massive hangar-type laboratory where astronauts trained on different types of systems. For example, there were real-size replicas of a docking apparatus. In this hangar were robot development projects. It was eerie to look at them and realize that we are trying to build robots that are designed to operate and think like humans. After the tram tour, I went into the only surviving full-size Boeing jet that was used to transport the Enterprise space shuttle prototype from California to Florida. On top of the Boeing jet was a mock-up of the space shuttle *Independence*.

Like my visit to the Kennedy Space Center, this Space Center Houston trip was so inspiring. The things humans can do when they work together is truly limitless! And more importantly, look at what can happen when the nations of the world work together. We get results, like the International Space Station — going strong after 20 years of operation — and we have the potential to get a person to Mars between 2035 and 2045. Not to mention all that was accomplished between the 1960s and 2011. From the Gemini missions to the last space shuttle launch, we have accomplished so much. I wonder what we would be doing if we kept up the drive we had in the 1960s, after President Kennedy challenged us to get to the moon before the end of the decade, "not because it is easy, but because it is hard."

On Wednesday, I traveled from Houston to Montgomery. This hearing had my youngest hearing client. He was a 30-year-old Black Iraq war veteran. His PTSD was rated at 70 percent, meaning he was almost "totally occupationally and socially impaired" because of his PTSD. I considered that we were in vastly different situations in life despite being only separated in age by three years.

I was so thrilled to hear this young man say that he has a strong support group between himself and other servicemen. He said they make it a point to share their feelings and help each other through tough times. So inspiring, and for men, unfortunately rarer than it should be.

The night before the hearing, I went to a great little country diner for dinner. This restaurant reminded me of Ridgetop back home in Maine and made me miss Grandma. I had chicken fried chicken for the first time ever. I was relieved to come home to Maine at the end of the day.

# FEBRUARY 2020

---

**FIRST WEEK OF FEBRUARY, 2020:** This week saw me take a fun swing through the South and began the densest month of travel I've ever had. Unknown to me at the time, it would also be my last full month on the road.

I started the weekend flying on Saturday, February 2, to Atlanta to spend the weekend with my high school friend, Eric, whom I last saw in September 2019. I had arranged to visit him because on Monday I had a hearing in Jackson, Mississippi, only 10 days since I had last visited that particular regional office.

I decided to stay in Atlanta with Eric through Super Bowl Sunday, as I did not relish the thought of watching it by myself in a hotel room or missing it because I was on a plane. I have never much cared for the game itself, but I value the night for its socialness and cultural importance.

Eric picked me up at the airport around 9 p.m., and we stayed up until 12 o'clock or so playing *Call of Duty* together. He is a fun friend to visit: up for anything and a conversationalist. I met for the first time his girlfriend, Erin, who is also a very nice and welcoming person.

The next morning, I grabbed brunch at a pancake place with Eric, Erin, and their friend, Jamie. This afforded me my first daylight impression of Atlanta. It was a beautiful day with little traffic, so my first impression was good. I remain in awe of the city infrastructure. It seems sprawling yet still built up. Eric and Erin lived on the northwest corner of the outer ring of the highway, near Marietta. So, they were not in city central, but they were close enough to still be considered living in bona fide Atlanta. The pancake place was closer to the city center in a historic part of their downtown.

After this, Eric and I went to the Jimmy Carter Presidential Museum. I really enjoyed this visit. I have admired Carter ever since I took a college Israeli-Palestinian conflict class. I admired Carter's attempt to broker a legitimate peace that satisfied both sides. Unlike some American politicians, I do not believe Carter was truly in one camp or another. He is also respectable for his considerable post-presidency activities — for which I believe he could truly be labeled as one of history's most dedicated human rights advocates. The museum was fairly small; it took Eric and I only about an hour and a half to go through.

That night, Eric and Erin had about eight of their friends over to watch the Super Bowl. Most were residents of the same apartment complex in which they lived. This complex had many units, and featured its own parking garage, mini-golf course, and dog park. It was an impressive place for sure and unlike anything I knew of in Maine. This night was one of those nights that made me really appreciate the opportunities my job has afforded me. Here I was amongst a group of people I did not know, but I felt more than welcomed and part of the crew. I definitely appreciated one of Eric's friends, Luke, coming over to me and trying to make conversation. I certainly did not feel like a wallflower and quickly assimilated myself with the group. The night was filled with conversation and laughter.

Indeed, only Eric was heavily invested in the game; everyone else was there for the socialization. I felt bad not being with my other friends for this occasion — for the past couple years I had gone over to Kyle and Mariah's to watch with that friend group. But this time I was thrilled to take advantage of my job to visit a friend and that the visit turned out so well. I felt so thankful to reconnect with a friend with whom I had fallen out of touch.

The game ended around midnight, and I left for the airport at around 5 a.m. on Monday morning. Eric walked me out as he had to let me out of the building, and I said I would try to see him again when I came back in April for NOVA's spring conference. Again, another plan destroyed by COVID.

I flew that morning to Jackson, Mississippi, as I had a hearing there at 12:30 p.m. I got to talk with Marie, the hearing coordinator. We remembered each other from when I was there just 10 days prior, and as it turns out, my client was able to have his hearing an hour and a half before the scheduled time. This was a simple, uncomplicated mental health claim. I was soon on my way in my rental car to Lafayette, where I had another hearing. I was looking forward to this long-planned drive from Jackson to Lafayette, as the drive was only three and half hours, yet through portions of the south where I had never been before. The driving route took the shape of a backwards "L." I proceeded down I-55, took a left at a junction in the highway, then drove the remaining hour or so through Baton Rouge and on to Lafayette. It was a beautiful day and nearly 75 degrees the entirety of the drive. I arrived in Lafayette around mid-afternoon and went for a much-needed run on the treadmill. I had a po' boy for dinner, figuring I had to if I was in the Deep South.

This was a hearing without a happy ending. I planned on basing my case on an earlier effective date for total disability, but the judge declined to address an earlier effective date for total disability (again, where a veteran is entitled to 100 percent of possible benefits provided by VA), as a separate appeal stream dealt with that issue. Therefore, the only issues I could talk about were those that were already subsumed within the current TDIU effective date, meaning no additional benefits could be received by the client — even if we were successful on the claims. However, I rationalized my error in not realizing that earlier effective date was not on appeal by drawing some good testimony on the issue of aid and attendance — an extra kind of compensation where the VA will award additional money if a veteran's service-connected disabilities exact a truly extraordinary toll on his daily life — which I stumbled into once the client started talking about how his wife takes care of most of his daily needs. Overall, I accepted responsibility for not realizing the true issues of the hearing, but think I mitigated my error in some way that helped the client. Still, I was embarrassed.

I then flew home for a much-appreciated four-day reprieve before my two weeks of near-constant travel.

By this time, Catherine and I had closed on a house in Sidney, about an hour and 15 minutes north of Jackson and MacNichol's office. We decided to move farther north to satiate my desire to be closer to my hometown and parents, while she still wanted to be close to Augusta and Waterville. This forced me to ask myself the question: How much longer did I see myself doing this job?

I thought long and hard, talking with family and friends. I concluded that, at that moment, the travel benefits of this job, *at this particular moment in my life*, outweighed the cons of not being home as much as I wanted. But now that I was getting married and buying a house, the pendulum was gradually balancing out toward looking for another job. Take away the novelty and growing fatigue of travel, and the balancing act shifted decisively to finding another job.

Such a reorientation has made me thankful that my February was so full. Now that I knew that my opportunities for travel might be voluntarily near an end, I was not so worked up over the fact that my February was jam-packed. This aligned with my general philosophy around my travels: live it up while I can!

**SECOND WEEK OF FEBRUARY, 2020:** This week was quite full. I left on Sunday to fly to Montgomery. I then went from Montgomery to Albuquerque, where I embarked on a 1,923-mile road trip around the Southwest!

The Montgomery hearing was typical. The visit was notable though because this was the first time I had spent some time in downtown Montgomery. I walked around downtown on Sunday night, so it was almost deserted. I stumbled across a statute of Rosa Parks, on the same corner where she boarded a bus and refused to go to the back of it. I had no idea this statue was here, but I was moved to come across it. The statue portrays her as a humble lady clutching a red rose.

On all my Lyft rides around town and to the airport, I had the same driver. His name was Johnny, and he was a great conversationalist. He gave me his cell phone number, so I could call him, and he could pick me up to get to the VA regional office and to the airport after my hearing. I enjoyed talking politics with him. As the reader can see, sometimes the most interesting people are those who drive Lyfts and Ubers.

On Monday night I flew to Albuquerque for a February 11 morning hearing. Thankfully, my client was able to go first, and we finished around 9 a.m. I was thrilled to be able to get out and start on my planned road trip to San Diego! I had a hearing there on February 13, and I had all afternoon of the 11th and all day on the 12th to get there. I would not have returned to Maine between hearings, so I made myself live to the fullest this visit to the Southwest.

The first leg of the trip was anticlimactic. Disappointedly, I drove in a driving snowstorm (yes, snow!) the entire way from Albuquerque to Tucson, Arizona. As soon as I hit the Arizona state line, however, the sky cleared, and I got a taste of the desert I was itching for.

I'll spare the reader my laborious attempts to describe the desert and what it means to me. I have done that plenty in previous journal entries. The stillness and vastness is so peaceful, soothing, and natural. I had not spent time in Arizona since I started this travel job, so I was thrilled to be in this classic desert setting.

I stopped in Tucson for the night and decided to go to a bar and grill close to my hotel. As soon as I walked in, I had one of the oddest experiences I've ever had in a restaurant. I went up to the bar, where an obviously drunk man named Kevin was annoying the waitress. He immediately turned around and started talking my ear off. He was way too friendly. He called over his "business partner," Precious, and the three of us stood together at the end of the bar for the entire time I was there. Kevin tried to explain that he was a screenwriter — he wanted to send me a screenplay of his to read — and alternatively suggested that he was some sort of psychic reader. He wanted to "talk with me" the next day, but there was obviously no way

I was going to do that. To be honest, I thought at one point he would try to proposition me, but nothing like that ever happened. He was out celebrating his birthday, which was the week before.

I left Tucson at sunrise the next day. I drove an hour and a half or so further south, to the Arizona/Mexico border, and hiked in the Organ Pipe National Monument. This was a national monument that featured thousands of cacti. I think they are so funny looking and had a blast driving through the monument. (A "monument" is a protected area declared so by the president; a "national park" is declared by Congress.)

I wanted to hike in this park, so I found a good trail on the map provided to me at the visitor center. It was an extraordinary day, 60 degrees and cloudless. I started on a trail that was described as only being .5 miles long. I was going to do this hike and another one up the loop road around the monument. However, when I got to the end of the advertised .5 miles, I discovered there was more to the route that could get me up to a rock archway. The full trail was explained on a sign as being 1.2 miles one way. I was up for the challenge and physical exercise after being in the car all day, so I proceeded up the rock face. I had a tough time getting up the mountain — maybe I just hadn't been on a desert hike in a while, or perhaps the hike was abnormally steep. But I did get to the top and was greeted by a magnificent view. Foolishly, I did not bring water or a snack bar. Also foolishly, I left the trail to try and get to the very top of a peak from which I thought I could see a more complete vista. Never, ever, leave the trail! As a result of my amateurish action, I lost the trail when I tried to find my way down the mountain. I stumbled around the mountainside for a couple hours — far more than I planned on taking to complete this hike — and all the while started to get light-headed from the lack of food or water. This was particularly dangerous because in my attempts to get down the mountain, I had to negotiate steep drops, essentially rock climb through some parts, and retrace my steps in order to find a safer way down. This was the first time I felt worried when on a hike. I was worried that I would slip and fall or get so dizzy as to fall off a steep rock face. I couldn't believe how stupid I was in not bringing water with me.

Ultimately, I was able to find the path again, and got back to my car. I determined that I had used all the time I could allow myself in this park and departed in order to keep my schedule of getting to San Diego by sundown.

The rest of the drive to San Diego was thrilling, too. Most notable was how closely I paralleled the Mexican border and all the border patrol cars I saw along the way across Arizona and southern California. As I crested the mountain range that absconds San Diego from the California interior, I was greeted by the setting sun. But because there were either clouds or fog, the red setting sun made the clouds look like they were on fire. It was an awe-inspiring, Biblical sight. I was driving where the fire clouds met the mountains. I wound my way around the mountains and arrived in San Diego just after the sun set.

I arrived at the hearing location in San Diego early enough to sign in my client first, meaning his hearing would be first. So I was able to leave quickly on Thursday morning and head back to Albuquerque. Like with all my road trips, I picked up and dropped off my rental car in the same place. Otherwise one-way fees piled up and made rental cars prohibitively expensive.

I decided I would stop in Phoenix for the night. I was impressed with southern California once I got outside of the city. I think I drove along what looked like the biggest mountain range I'd ever seen. At the very least, I was very close to this range as I drove east. I drove through an idyllic little town surrounded by mountains. It's amazing how diverse California is!

I spent a lot of time this trip talking to Grandad, who was thrilled to follow my progress as I crossed the desert. He lived in Tucson for a time and earned his master's degree there. He was enthralled with the desert for the same reasons I was. He said if he was young again, he would do exactly what I was doing. I drove into Phoenix around sundown, as planned, and was anxious to devote some time to getting some work done and talk with Catherine, as I did every night I was away from home.

On Friday, I left Phoenix. I decided to make two stops on my way to Albu-querque. The first was in Winslow, Arizona, which is now famous because of the Eagles song "Take it Easy." Downtown they had a small park called Standing on the Corner park, named after the song lyric. This park was very cool to visit. The town obviously took pride in their fame. There was even a flatbed Ford parked on the street and statues of two Eagles band members — one of whom was Glenn Frey. Overall, this was a great detour.

I then proceeded to the Petrified Forest National Park, located about half-way between Flagstaff and Albuquerque. Judging from my cursory internet research before visiting, I expected a quick visit to view the "painted des-ert," for which this region of Arizona is famous. However, I spent nearly three hours in the park. This region was a kind of badlands that, due to various geological abnormalities, makes the rock look spongy, porous, and tinted blue and purple. Exploring the park consisted of driving along a 10-mile driving route, where along the way I would get out to look at various points of interest.

One of the most striking exhibits was an ancient Pueblo settlement, dated to be at least 700 years old. Examining these ruins was moving. These ruins were of a 100-room settlement — a kind of stopping point along a trading route that formed because this settlement was at the confluence of two major rivers. I tried to envision what life was like here 700 years ago. The rooms were made of clay; days were devoted to village upkeep and cultural activities, such as drawing petroglyphs, of which some were still visible on nearby rock faces. I was amazed at how these drawings could be seen today. What did they represent? Petroglyphs do not represent language; rather, they were pictorial images, kind of like a children's book where illustrations are the primary way of telling a story. I am enthralled with history, so one can imagine how excited I was to explore these ruins.

The last stop on the driving route was exploring the Blue Mesa. This was an area of the aforementioned blue badlands. A walking trail took me down to the base of a particular group of these rock formations. It looked like the rock was very cold because they were so bluish-purple. They were spongy to the touch! Quite fascinating. I explored all this against the backdrop of a beautiful day. Some of the views were jaw-dropping. At one point one could pull over to the side of the road and look at a mountain that was labeled by a sign as being 108 miles away.

Finally, I should explain why the park is called the "petrified forest." There are no trees to be found, at least living ones. Instead, dotting the brown landscape are rock-like petrified trees. These trees were encased in mud and preserved over the hundreds of years, such that they feel like rock, but they were once regular trees.

Overall, this visit turned out to be one of the highlights of my trip, even though I only planned it to be a quick stop near the end of my journey. These are the best kinds of experiences. I left the petrified forest with a deep sense of satisfaction. I arrived in Albuquerque later that evening. According to my Avis email receipt, I covered 1,923 miles in only four days. This does not match the density of travel I did on my 2017-2018 cross-country road trip, but it certainly takes the prize for longest road trip since I started this job. I was thrilled to mark this trip on my map when I got home. I was able to enjoy a brief, one-day respite at home before I embarked on my next trip.

This trip turned out to be the return to the desert I had been looking forward to. However, I did reach a threshold decision during this trip. I decided the cons of all this travel are starting to outweigh the pros. I missed home and Catherine too much. I figured this trip would allow me to "go out with a bang." I thought it was telling that as much as I love getting to places I normally would never have an opportunity to go, I started to desire the opportunity to be at home more than anything else. As always, I miss Catherine, my friends, family, and the routine of a normal life when I am traveling. However, up until now, the benefit of travel has outweighed the cons. Perhaps part of the scales flipping on me comes from the fact that we are soon closing on a house. Regardless, I knew my feelings were valid *and* particularly probative coming in the middle of a fun desert road trip. It took eight months of heavy travel, but I finally got to the point of saying my desire to be home outweighed my desire to travel for work.

I emailed Jack, asking him to take me off the roster of travel attorneys. I felt self-centered making such a request — after all, I was hired as a *traveling* attorney — but I felt this was the right course of action. There was plenty of in-office work to do for attorneys, and a couple of my co-workers had already been reassigned to be in-house attorneys.

Surprisingly, Jack respected but denied this request. I didn't blame him; the logistics of pulling an attorney out of the travel rotation would have been awful. I started actively looking for other in-state jobs. It killed me to do so, but I felt that was the best course of action.

**THIRD WEEK OF FEBRUARY, 2020:** This week saw me take another, albeit shorter, trip through a different part of the desert. On Monday, President's Day, I left Portland, Maine, for Salt Lake City. Over Monday and Tuesday, I drove from Salt Lake City to Elko, Nevada, then to Winnemucca, Nevada, from which I shot north through southeastern Oregon, to Boise, Idaho, where I had a hearing on Wednesday morning.

This wasn't the kind of desert like I experienced in the southwest, but it was notable nonetheless. These mountains were snowcapped and seemingly more sprawling. I kept thinking that I was driving through a painting. I drove a couple hours after landing in Salt Lake City, ending my night in Elko, Nevada. I left at sunrise the next morning, driving west until I reached Winnemucca and turning north to drive along a state route up through southeastern Oregon. I was fascinated to see this part of Oregon. This was more typical desert. Certainly not what I was expecting given how lush and green western Oregon is. I continued up through Oregon until I stopped for lunch about seven miles from the Idaho border. I landed in Idaho in the early afternoon, affording me an opportunity to go on the treadmill and have a relaxing late afternoon. The 32-degree weather precluded any outdoor activity.

My hearing the next morning was in downtown Boise. I was able to finish this hearing by around 10 a.m. and, therefore, had to fill the rest of my day. Unfortunately, it was too cold to go hiking, and people told me that the trails around Boise were muddy due to recent rain. Therefore, I could not really do anything outdoors. I did walk around downtown Boise for a short time after my hearing, grabbing a cup of coffee and lunch before going back to the hotel. I spent the remainder of the day doing work. I was sad that I could not take advantage of being among some Rocky Mountains; they tantalizingly sat with their majestic peaks, just on the outskirts of the city.

My hearing concerned a homeless client. It's important to note that "homeless" does not necessarily mean living on the street. Instead, the VA defines "homeless" as what we would colloquially call "couch surfing," living in a homeless shelter, rapidly moving between housing situations, or having an unsure housing situation. This client passionately conveyed to me and the judge how difficult his fight was with the VA, made even harder by not knowing where he was going to live in any given week. I realized that homelessness is such a pressing issue for veterans, who sometimes cannot hold any work because of their disabilities. That is why I decided that at least half of my profits from this book will go to a holistic, national, and effective veterans' charity, which tackles all veterans' issues, including homelessness. The Disabled American Veterans (DAV) fit the bill.

The next day, I left Boise to go to St. Louis. This week was unusual in that I went to two different hearing locations I had never been to before and two states I had not been to before while in this job.

St. Louis was interesting. Shortly after getting to my hotel, I walked around the St. Louis Arch, which was very close to my hotel in downtown St. Louis. This structure was remarkable. It was much bigger than I envisioned it. An elevator took visitors to the top, but I did not have any interest in going up. Walking around the area of the arch, I also discovered a plaque that commemorated the westernmost battle of the American Revolution, right there in downtown St. Louis. It was also bitterly cold in St. Louis, so I could not stay outside for long.

The next day, my hearing went smoothly, but it was marked by my client's and my time waiting for our hearing to start. Another veteran was waiting for his attorney to show up, but when he did, they got into an awful shouting match with each other, such that security had to be called. Clients exploding at attorneys is not exactly unheard of, but it was very unprofessional for the attorney to engage, as well.

My attention now turned to my excitement at visiting my German friend, Leon. I left St. Louis on Friday night, arriving in Greenville, South Carolina, at 5:30 p.m.

The weekend that followed was a blast. Leon picked me up at the airport. He and I first met when I lived with his family for two weeks in April 2011, in Pulheim, Germany. Despite only knowing each other for a couple weeks, we became fast friends and stayed in intermittent touch throughout the 2010s. In 2019 he came to Maine for his first ever Thanksgiving. This was the first time I had seen him in seven years — since 2012 when I lived in Germany and visited him for a weekend in his hometown of Pulheim. For the last six months, he has lived in South Carolina, taking an internship with BMW. After Thanksgiving, I resolved to try as hard as I could to visit him before he left the United States on March 20. February 22 and 23 were two of the only dates available to me, so I readily jumped at the opportunity.

He picked me up, and we went back to his apartment, where he lived with another German, Ottum. I rank Leon with College Bill as a natural conversationalist. Whenever we see each other, we are constantly communicating. We love learning about our respective, shared cultures (my maternal grandmother was 100 percent German). We also both endorsed the idea that *by learning about each other we learn about ourselves*. We are naturally inquisitive and friendly, making a perfect match when we first were paired through my high school's German-American partnership exchange program.

Friday night Leon made goulash for dinner. He remembered me telling him that my German grandmother used to make that for Kyle and me when we were kids. This was very sweet of him to do. Then, we went with a few of his friends to a nearby apartment party, hosted by some of Leon's work friends. I was thrilled to meet other Germans! We "pre-gamed" at a nearby apartment of Leon's closer friends. They were named Kai, Alex, and Daniel, the latter who was actually a Mexican. Other Germans I met included David, who was so tall I only came up to his chin, and a couple German women. This was the first time in a long while I had been to a college-like party, and to be honest, I felt a bit out of place. I was the oldest person there, except for another German who was only two days older than me, and everyone else was 22 or 23. Despite the age difference, I had a few drinks and enjoyed meeting some of Leon's friends.

Saturday morning was slow, but Leon and I were perfectly content. We watched Bundesliga soccer games (German soccer), made more fun by the fact that Leon's team, Cologne, played Berlin, which I felt a passing loyalty for due to living in Berlin during the summer of 2012. We also watched a couple episodes of *South Park* with his roommate.

After the game, we went to Leon's friends' apartment and played a fun German card game called *Wizard*, based on ancient German folklore. When we started, Kai asked me in his very thick German accent what kind of music I liked. I answered Elton John as an example, and he put on Elton's Spotify profile. I remarked that there was actually a song by Elton about a German border crossing guard who fell in love with a West Berliner. This is Elton's 1985 song called "Nikita," off the album *Ice on Fire*. He gave me the phone to put on the song, and I picked the album version. To my surprise, nobody moved to change the music after the song ended, so it made an awesome memory for me to be sitting playing this fun card game and listening to the entirety of *Ice on Fire*. The game was full of laughs, and I actually did not do too badly. I picked it up quickly.

David, the Mexican roommate, made everyone soft-shell tacos for dinner. After this we wanted to go to a driving range, but a prohibitively long wait made us go bowling instead. Leon rallied other friends of his, meaning that we went bowling with three Americans (including me), five Germans, three Brazilians, and one Mexican. Anyone who knows my passion for meeting and learning about other cultures can probably guess how thrilled I was to socialize with these people.

After the game, we did go back to the apartment and socialize more. Others came over, and Leon and I got involved in a conversation with one of the Brazilian women. She was fascinating and provided nice insight into her life in Brazil before coming to America to also work at BMW (all these foreign students worked at BMW). Leon and I stayed awake until 12:30 a.m.; we got so engaged with these post-bowling conversations. One of the Brazilians boldly asked the Germans how they are taught Nazism in school; Kai and Leon responded unoffended. Not being offended by anything is the key to learning about other people, especially as you try to learn from others by asking them questions. Again, that is another reason why Leon and I get along so well. One of the first things I told him, and tell others, is that "nothing offends me."

Sunday was memorable as well. If Saturday and Friday were about socializing with Leon's friends, Sunday was all about Leon and I. We awoke around 9:30 again and watched a soccer game. After this, we headed downtown until I had to get to the airport around 3:30 p.m. We went to lunch at a Cajun restaurant, then walked around downtown Greenville. I was impressed with Greenville; it had a downtown Bar Harbor feel, but thank God it was not as crowded. It featured an amphitheater and a river walk over a waterfall. We found a Starbucks and sat outside, people watching and talking about anything that popped into our head. We reminisced about Thanksgiving. Leon said some things that stuck with me. He said that he was affected by my grandmother's death more than he thought he would be. He remembered meeting her in the fall of 2011 and fondly noted that she would write to him on Facebook from time to time, and he remembered watching a high school football game with her. He even remembered that everyone called Grandma "Mustang Sally" (my high school mascot was a Mustang). He recalled Thanksgiving as "perfect." He remarked that he was so excited for Clara, his girlfriend, to meet Catherine and me. It's hard to believe that this was only the fourth time we had seen each other face to face. I am not surprised that it feels like I have known him for much longer. I remember remarking to him at the end of my first visit that, "Even though we have known each other for 13 days, I feel like I've known you for 13 years." Such was our ability to become fast friends.

He dropped me off at the airport. We took solace in that this was not a big goodbye, as we had standing plans to see each other when Catherine and I traveled to Germany as part of our July 2020 honeymoon. Again, COVID rendered this not the case.

I arrived in Portland at 11 p.m. On my way to my apartment, which was only four miles away from the airport, my car's lights flickered. Its odometer crashed, and RPMs flatlined to zero. Confused, I pulled over, turned off the car, and thought a restart might solve the problem. The car never started again. There I was, thrilled to be *almost* home, so close yet so far! I tried calling Catherine, but it was 11:30 p.m., and she was fast asleep. I called the police and informed them of a car on the side of the road. The police officer who showed up was incredibly nice and drove me the remaining mile and a half to my apartment.

I was so excited to return home. I had spent only one day in Maine over the past two weeks. Part of the density of this travel was my own doing, but I did know regardless of whose fault it was, work's or mine, I knew that this travel journal would probably soon come to an end. Buying a house, living farther away from the airport, missing my life in Maine — these factors combined to really make me look unfavorably on new hearing assignments. I hope the reader can see that I truly appreciated the opportunities afforded in this job — something I feel is a common theme throughout this travel journal — but the fact remains that I wanted to settle down more. If I went to only one or two hearings every couple of weeks, the situation would be different. But such would probably never be the case.

SPRING

# MARCH 2020 AND AN ABRUPT END

**FIRST WEEK OF MARCH, 2020:** This week was the first time I went to four different cities in four days. Sunday night saw me fly out to Chicago, then fly the next day to Des Moines. Wednesday I was home, and then Thursday I left early in the morning for Baltimore. From Baltimore I went to New Orleans for a Friday hearing.

I'll admit I was too terrified to go out in Chicago to do any exploring. I knew the reputation, rightly or wrongly, it had for violence. Was this feeling valid for where I was staying? Maybe. Maybe not. Regardless, I let my fear neuter my desire to explore. I also arrived in town later in the evening, so I was content with just doing work in my hotel. My hearing went well, but then I accidently went to the wrong airport after the hearing. I had the Lyft driver take me to O'Hare, not Midway, so I arrived at Midway with only 40 minutes or so before my flight. That was the first time that had ever happened!

My visit to Des Moines was similarly brief and to the point. In Des Moines Monday night, I went to a German restaurant near my hotel, called Hessan Haus. Hessan is a city in Germany (actually where Leon's grandfather is from), and "*haus*" is "house" in German. Also notable was that one of my Des Moines' Lyft drivers was intensely curious to learn I was a veteran's disability attorney, as he was actively dealing with getting VA benefits. These kind of encounters reinforced one of the reasons I decided to write this book: everyone knows a veteran.

I was home on Wednesday, which was only the second day ever that I worked from home. It was certainly a precursor of things to come. I sold my alternatively beloved and reviled 2009 Chevy Cobalt. This Cobalt had been giving me many problems recently, and I decided it was too old and unreliable to keep dumping more money into. I have many fond memories of it: taking me on my cross-country road trip and all around Maine, Quebec, and the East Coast, etc. But I had to be practical and recognize it was time to get a new car.

On Wednesday, a threshold event happened. While I was working from home, I finally learned how to request multipoint hearings from "Togus," the term for Maine's VA regional office. This was an assignment of which Jack put me in charge. Essentially, the firm's policy thus far had been to go out to meet the veteran at their regional office, and then face the judge together. However, in-office work and fears of the new coronavirus threat meant that Jack wanted the travel attorneys to travel less. The most practical option, then, would be to have the hearing attorneys in Togus and video link with the veteran at the regional office and the judge in Washington, DC. This means that the new normal will be for me to have my hearings in Togus, and only rarely travel out of state. At this particular moment in time, I felt relieved that I would become a little more settled. I knew, however, that I would miss the travel after I spent a few weeks in the office. But as I said, the balancing act had turned such that I needed to prioritize being home more, over having adventures out of state — no matter how much I ended up missing it. To this end, on Wednesday I scheduled my March 20 Los Angeles hearing to be a multipoint hearing out of Togus and scheduled my March 26 St. Louis hearing to be out of Togus.

Despite these growing fears of a virus, on Thursday, I went to Baltimore early in the morning, had my hearing at 12:30, then flew in the evening to New Orleans. I had never been to the Baltimore location before, and I didn't have much of an opportunity to explore, as I did not stay in town overnight. I also understand Baltimore has a reputation for violence and crime, so I probably would not have felt excited about going out anyway. My client showed up wearing a surgical mask, as the coronavirus threat had started taking Americans' attention by storm.

My New Orleans hearing was similarly unmemorable. I stayed in a hotel closer to the airport, as I flew in fairly late at night. I was able to get home that same night at around 12:30 in the morning. When I returned home, that Friday night was the last night in the Westbrook apartment. Catherine and I moved into our new house in Sidney the next day, March 7, which was the day after our two-year dating anniversary.

**SECOND WEEK OF MARCH, 2020:** This week only saw me go to Waco, Texas, but it was notable as the end of my heavy hearing travel. The trip was unremarkable. I elected to say in Maine for most of the day on Tuesday and flew out of Portland at 4 p.m. I arrived in Dallas at around 10 p.m. and immediately went to my hotel. I picked my rental car up in the morning and headed to Waco for my 12:30 hearing. This was a good case to go out on — total disability possible to at least 2013 or 2010. Waco must be in the running for the place I have had a plurality of my hearings. Waco must also hold the title for hardest place to get to. At least two flights are required, only then those flights get me into Dallas, where I have to rent a car for the hour-and-forty-five-minute-long trip to Waco. This drive, while on the highway, is mired by construction, producing congestion and confusion. Waco itself is a nightmare to try and get around.

I flew home later that evening and arrived in Sidney around 1 a.m. This was the first time I had to go to Sidney and not Westbrook. Thank God the hearing travel was over. Sidney is at least an hour away from the airport.

On March 11, I wrote the summation to this journal on my way home to Portland. I wrote that I thought my heavy travel might end for a month due to the coronavirus. When this book went to print in fall 2020 I was still exclusively working from home.

On March 13, Jack gathered all the firm's attorneys and announced our response to the coronavirus. All attorneys were to work from home and leave the office immediately. In the course of one meeting, my life went from never being home, to never leaving home. One moment I was always out "there," and in an instance permanently "back again." Like for billions of people around the world, the virus changed the course of my life. Such radical change was difficult to adapt to. I cannot give enough credit to the VA, however, for so quickly rolling out a "video conference" prototype program where veterans could have their hearings on their computers or smartphones. My job radically changed, but I still had a job. I was far luckier than millions of people and quite a few of my close friends.

Do I miss the thrill of travel? Of course, every day. My wanderlust grows with suddenly nowhere to go. There are so many other, unexplored interesting places in the world. But do I miss the *density* of travel? Absolutely not. If I had a choice between always being home, or never being home, I would choose the former in a heartbeat. I do miss meeting my clients in person, putting a face to a name. I "meet" them on the phone and in video conferences, but that's not the same, or as memorable, as meeting them in person.

I spent the flight home on March 11 further reflecting on the opportunities and experiences recalled in the preceding pages. My heart swells and my eyes glisten at the thought of all that I have done over these nine months. The people I have met, the places I've seen, the lessons I've learned, and the lives I have touched and that have touched me. In a good way, it is all overwhelming. I wrote that in 11 days, on March 21, I would turn 27 years old. No one — particularly at my age — has a right to experience all that I have.

Furthermore, I reaffirmed my decision in accepting this job right after law school, a view I know I have mentioned in preceding entries. I frequently state how I would have not have taken any other job right after law school. Man, what a good decision.

Thinking back on the places I've been, my favorite place was Wyoming, followed closely by the New Mexico/Arizona desert. But perhaps most of all, my favorite part was meeting people — meeting my clients who affected my life as much as I affected theirs, as well as the strangers who gave my life some context. They had their own valuable lessons to impart on me.

I am also thankful that the VA affords veterans the option of a hearing — an opportunity borne out of anyone's constitutional right to "procedural due process." Much healing — both emotional and financial — has come from these hearings. As I stated in the prologue, I attended about 77 of these over the course of my travel. Of all the numbers I've cited, however, I am most proud of "0": the number of hearings and flights I missed because of my own negligence.

Finally, I am thankful that I decided to keep this journal. It will bring great joy and recollection throughout the rest of my life. I already want to go back and re-read some entries, look back and relive some of the most fun parts of my nine months exploring America.

I hope you, the reader, apply my story to your own life — find what you are thankful for, find the perspective that makes you feel truly lucky to be alive, or get the bug to go out and explore the world. In so doing, you'll perhaps find out more about yourself than the world around you. This might be the whole idea in the first place.